"What has become of the steed?

What has become of the warrior?

What has become of the seats of banquet?

Where are the joys of the hall?

O for the bright cup!

O for the mailclad warrior!

O for the glory of the prince!

How that time has passed away

And grown dark under the cover of night,

As if it had never been."

—FROM "THE WANDERER,"
ANONYMOUS ANGLO-SAXON POEM

Riding out a storm, Viking merchant-marauders lash down their goods and weapons

THE VIKINGS

By Howard La Fay

Photographed by Ted Spiegel

Illustrated by Louis S. Glanzman

Foreword by Arne Emil Christensen, Jr.

Prepared by

The Special Publications Division,

National Geographic Society,

Washington, D. C.

The Norse ships handled well even in heavy seas.

THE VIKINGS
By HOWARD LA FAY
National Geographic
  Foreign Editorial Staff
Photographed by TED SPIEGEL
Illustrated by LOUIS S. GLANZMAN

Published by
THE NATIONAL GEOGRAPHIC SOCIETY
MELVIN M. PAYNE, *President*
MELVILLE BELL GROSVENOR,
  Editor-in-Chief
GILBERT M. GROSVENOR, *Editor*

Prepared by
THE SPECIAL PUBLICATIONS DIVISION
ROBERT L. BREEDEN, *Editor*
DONALD J. CRUMP, *Associate Editor*
PHILIP B. SILCOTT, *Senior Assistant Editor*
MERRILL WINDSOR, *Managing Editor*
WILLIAM R. GRAY, ELIZABETH C. WAGNER,
  Assistants to the Editor
MARJORIE W. CLINE, ELIZABETH C.
  WAGNER, *Research*

Illustrations
DAVID R. BRIDGE, *Picture Editor*
MARGERY G. DUNN, RONALD M. FISHER,
  STRATFORD C. JONES, JOHN S.
  GRAHAM, *Picture Legends*
MARJORIE W. CLINE, *Picture Legend*
  Research

Design and Art Direction
JOSEPH A. TANEY, *Art Director*
JOSEPHINE B. BOLT, *Associate Art Director*
URSULA PERRIN, *Design Assistant*
PAUL M. BREEDEN, *Calligraphy*
JOHN D. GARST, JR., LISA BIGANZOLI,
  MONICA W. LEBEAU, *Map Research and*
  Production

Production and Printing
ROBERT W. MESSER, *Production Manager*
MARGARET MURIN SKEKEL, RAJA D.
  MURSHED, *Production Assistants*
JAMES R. WHITNEY, JOHN R. METCALFE,
  Engraving and Printing

MARTA I. BERNAL, SUZANNE J.
  JACOBSON, ELIZABETH VAN BEUREN
  JOY, JOAN PERRY, *Staff Assistants*

BRIT AABAKKEN PETERSON, VIRGINIA S.
  THOMPSON, *Index*

Standard Book Number 87044-108-6
Library of Congress Catalog Card Number
  72-75383

*Page 1: Chessman of walrus ivory survives
from the 12th century. Endpapers: Runestones
offer enigmatic glimpses of the Viking past.
Bookbinding: Intrepid Norsemen depart on a
voyage of exploration.*

PAGE 1: COURTESY TRUSTEES OF THE BRITISH MUSEUM;
ENDPAPERS: LÄRBRO, GOTLAND, SWEDEN. (STONE ON LEFT
STANDS 11.4 FEET HIGH, THE OTHER 8.3 FEET)

Contents

*Blonde hair set aglow by the northern sun, Ing-Marie
Nöjd watches as competitors cross the finish line
during a race in the Småland Highlands of Sweden.*

Foreword

Why does the distant Viking Age capture the imagination of scholars and laymen alike, and why can more and more books be written about this rather short period of the European past?

The Vikings—Scandinavian raiders, merchants, and settlers of the 9th to 11th centuries—came out of a dark North that left us few historic sources. Annals and sagas from Byzantium to Iceland tell of their deeds, but written records of that time are rare in the Norse homelands.

But spectacular archeological discoveries over many years have made it possible to piece together a vivid picture of what life in the Viking Age was like. Ranging from the humble tools of the yeoman farmer to 95-foot Viking ships and the remains of precisely-constructed military camps, the finds are richer in number and scope than those of any other period of northern prehistory.

Since 1961 the excavations of Helge Ingstad in Newfoundland have finally proved Norse settlement in the New World around A.D. 1000, and have renewed public interest in the Vikings on both sides of the Atlantic.

When I first met Howard La Fay, he was writing a GEOGRAPHIC story on the Vikings—an article received with such interest by Society members, I am told, that it led to the decision to publish this book. He came to see me about the Northmen's ships, my own special field, and I immediately envied him his rare opportunity to follow in the wake of the Vikings virtually everywhere they had gone. As our association continued, my envy grew. Many volumes have been written on the Viking Age, but I know of no author who has himself gone a-viking so far and wide as Howard La Fay.

The Society's tradition of telling a story with pictures has resulted in a remarkable set of illustrations for this book, both photographs and paintings. Much labor has gone into the effort to recapture Viking Age scenes. In many cases, source material was vague or nonexistent, and sometimes one of several interpretations had to be chosen. I hope and believe that the pictures will convey to readers the splendor and drama of the period, and that departures from any school of opinion will stimulate future research.

Present excavations in the Viking towns of Dublin and Hedeby offer much for further study, and a steady flow of new material broadens museum collections all over Scandinavia. Historians, too, are taking renewed interest in the limited written sources of the period. At the same time, practical experiments in reliving some aspects of Viking Age culture are undertaken on an increasing scale, especially in Denmark, where volunteers—working with archeologists and using the old methods—build Viking ships and reconstruct Viking houses. Despite all the difficulties they face, this "experimental archeology" will surely teach us a great deal about the life and craftsmanship of a thousand years ago that could never be deduced from artifacts and sagas alone. And with every increase in our knowledge, the Viking Age grows more fascinating.

ARNE EMIL CHRISTENSEN, JR., Curator
University Museum of National Antiquities, Oslo

*C*hill *stream cascades toward Norway's Hjørund Fjord. From such misty harbors the Vikings set forth to explore, plunder, and trade.*

FURY OUT OF THE NORTH

AN INTRODUCTION

s the eighth century of the Christian Era waned, the people of western Europe inhabited a relatively secure and ordered world. On all sides stood the crumbling relics of the great empire that had died 300 years before; but after the prolonged strife and turmoil that attended the fall of Rome, the populace had finally found a kind of peace amid the ruins. Farmers, craftsmen, and monks followed their respective callings to the slow, sure rhythm of early medieval life.

Until A.D. 793.

On the eighth day of June of that year, "the harrying of the heathen miserably destroyed God's church in Lindisfarne by rapine and slaughter." That terse statement in the Anglo-Saxon Chronicle marks the explosion of the Vikings into the mainstream of history.

The heathen who sacked the small tidal island off Britain's east coast had sailed across the North Sea in unstable ships with perilously little freeboard. Their homes lay far to the forbidding north, in lands untouched by Christianity. From the prows of their delicate, singularly beautiful vessels glared fanciful heads of horses and serpents and dragons. Their feat of navigation astounded Europeans whose world ceased almost at the shoreline; so did their barbarous conduct. "Never before," wailed the scholar Alcuin, "has such a terror appeared in Britain."

Those first Vikings, in the words of Alcuin, "desecrated the sanctuaries of God, and poured out the blood of saints around the altar, laid waste the house of our hope, trampled on the bodies of saints in the temple of God." The raid on Lindisfarne set the pattern for centuries of pillage. Harassing all the coasts of Europe, Vikings ravished women, murdered babes, took countless slaves. They looted sacred ornaments and vestments, plundered libraries that preserved the last literary legacies of the ancient world. What they could not carry off, they wantonly burned.

To a Europe "adorned with churches as the sky with stars," all peace ended with the arrival of these bearded giants who worshiped strange gods and avidly sought glory in death rather than serenity in life. So ceaseless and fierce became their depredations that congregations throughout western Christendom prayed: "*A furore Normannorum libera nos, Domine* — From the fury of the Northmen deliver us, O Lord!"

To be sure, the Vikings were cruel; but so was the time. On their enemies they sometimes inflicted a hideous and terminal torture called "the blood eagle": Splitting a man's back, they would pull out his lungs so that, with his last gasps, they flapped like crimson wings. On the other hand, when a Viking raid on Seville ended in disaster, all the trees of that great city hardly sufficed to hang the host of captured Norsemen. As souvenirs of his victory, the Moorish Emir Abd al-Rahman sent 200 blond Viking heads to his counterpart in Tangier.

And when Basil II, Emperor of Byzantium — the most civilized state of that day — defeated the Bulgarians in 1014, he took some 14,000 captives. Basil blinded them, but left each hundredth man with one eye. He then dispatched

Near their farmstead on Hjørund Fjord, Jetmund Skår balances his oars while Stein, 16, trolls with a hand line. Like their Viking forebears, the Skårs fish and farm: Jetmund's wife, Borghild, milks one of their goats.

W*hetting the short scythe Norsemen have used for centuries on rocky slopes, Karsten Skår—Jetmund Skår's brother-in-law—prepares to cut winter forage. He farms 7 acres of cleared land bordering Jetmund's 12; just inland rise the mountains. Their holdings, typically small in a region of limited tillable land, yield hay, grain, and vegetables. Farther north, farmers depend more on livestock than on crops.*

the wretched prisoners back to their leader in detachments of 100, each with a one-eyed man as guide.

The foray at Lindisfarne marked a bloody preamble to the Viking Age — more than 250 years of turbulence and dread; years, too, I learned as I sought the remains of that roughhewn era, of discovery and colonization; years of epic heroism, epic poetry, and epic tragedy.

The origin of the word that gave the age its name, *Viking*, lies lost in the past. Etymologists speculate that it might derive from the Old Norse *vik*, meaning a fjord-like inlet, or from *vig*, battle. Historical sources attest only that it gained currency as a verb rather than a noun, and that throughout Scandinavia "to go viking" came to mean quite simply to embark on an expedition of piracy and plunder.

As the ninth century dawned, Swedes, Danes, and Norwegians surged out of their frosty fastness at the top of Europe in a giant, ever-advancing pincers that eventually encompassed the continent. Merchants as well as warriors, they traded as often as they raided; and with increasing frequency as the years passed, they settled on the sites of their conquests.

In the East, Swedish Vikings — greedy for the exotic wares of Araby — funneled down wild, uncharted Russian rivers into the Black and Caspian Seas. They ruled in Novgorod, founded a dynasty in Kiev, and even dared to attack the mightiest of cities, Constantinople. Their valor so impressed the Byzantine rulers that they recruited Northmen into an elite military unit that for centuries, as the famed Varangian Guard, protected the person of the emperor at home and served as imperial shock troops in the field.

In the West, Danes and Norwegians probed every island and inlet and stream from the North Sea to Spain in search of booty and trade goods. Viking fleets battered London Bridge, besieged Paris, burned mosques in Andalusia, and took slaves in North Africa. They harried in the Mediterranean, sailed up the Rhône to sack Arles, raided Pisa, and may even have dropped anchor in Egypt's fabled harbor of Alexandria.

In western France, Viking bands occupied the lands they had ravaged. There they sired a new breed of men, the Normans, who radically altered the course of history. One of them, William the Bastard, conquered England in 1066, completely disrupted the native Anglo-Saxon civilization, and left an imprint on language, culture, and government that endures to this day.

History abounds in ironies. Carved on the wall of an ancient church in the Norman town of Dives-sur-Mer are the names of those hardy few who accompanied William to find lands and glory in England. Among them are Hugue and Roger de Montgommeri. Almost 900 years later, in June of 1944, at a beach near Arromanches a scant 25 miles from Dives, a namesake returned to Normandy. He was General Sir Bernard Law Montgomery, commander of the Allied armies that had stormed ashore to free Europe from Nazi tyranny.

In perhaps the greatest exploit of the Middle Ages, eight sons of an obscure Norman knight, Tancred de Hauteville, went viking — overland, in this case — to southern Italy and Sicily where they founded the most aggressive and splendid kingdom of its time. Other Normans joined the Crusades and, ever greedy for land, these descendants of Vikings carved out fiefdoms along the coasts of the Near East.

Viking seafarers had always displayed a strong interest in exploring the unknown, but extensive voyages were limited by the relative fragility of their early vessels. As Viking power waxed, however, so did the quality of their ships and their seamanship.

Copernicus had not yet revolutionized knowledge of the universe, and virtually everyone viewed the world as flat, with the gray mystery of the North Atlantic ending in a turmoil of monsters. Beyond that lay the void. Most mariners, fearing certain calamity beyond the horizon, never willingly left the sight of land. Yet generations of Norse skippers pressed relentlessly toward the sunset. In the bleak oceanic waste, they colonized the Orkneys, the Shetlands, the Faeroes, the Hebrides, Iceland, Greenland. Shortly before the year 1000, adverse winds blew a young Greenland-bound captain, Bjarni Herjulfsson, past his destination. Farther west than any European before him, he skirted the coast of a new land "well-wooded and with low hills" — America.

In their long and restless voyaging, a few Viking sailors developed navigational techniques and instruments of startling sophistication, including a *solarstein* — or sunstone — that enabled a mariner to locate the sun through an overcast. In its function, the sunstone duplicated the twilight compass that now guides great jet aircraft across the polar cap.

My own exploration of the Vikings' world revealed its vastness and its infinite variety. I saw the remains of their dwellings and boat sheds beside piney Newfoundland forests. I sailed in their wake along the windswept shores of the Caspian Sea. I followed them from the long Arctic nights of Iceland to the soft breezes of the Bosporus. And I duly found their faint traces — runic inscriptions, crumbled longhouses, magnificently resurrected ships of war.

I found too a spiritual heritage, one common to all mankind, but perhaps best realized among the long-dead Norsemen. Once, in the tenth century, a Frankish messenger on the banks of the Eure hailed a Viking band sailing up that French river.

"Who is your master?" he demanded.

"None," came the reply. "We are all equals."

Until recently, most historians dismissed the Northmen as little more than raiders on a grand scale. This opinion stemmed largely from the works of Christian chroniclers who, understandably enough, portrayed the pagans at their worst. Now, however, evidence indicates that the Vikings were formidable merchants. They bartered furs and slaves for the luxuries of southern and eastern climes, and their commercial journeys put them in contact with the farthest reaches of the known world. Precious objects from China and India have come to light in tenth-century Swedish hoards and graves.

Indeed, in a day when Christian Europe was an inward-looking, parochial congeries of petty states, the Northmen were remarkably cosmopolitan. At the pinnacle of Norse power, a Viking could journey to Rouen or Dublin, to

W*hen autumn temperatures drop, Karsten Skår begins the slaughter*
of goats for the winter table. He carries a carcass into the storehouse
to hang for several days before he cuts and salts the meat.

In an open-sided boat shed on the fjord, wood pegging of an ancient
construction method used as late as 1900 weathers the years.

Brothers-in-law talk beside Skaar hamlet pier. At Karsten's farm his wife, Karen, lifts the traditional thin bread lefse, rolled and ready to fry; Freydis, 6, shapes more dough. Jetmund's son Bjørn, 13, studies a tape recorder, product of an outside world many Norwegian farmers' sons must join; customarily the elder sons inherit the farms, and the younger leave to find careers elsewhere.

Novgorod or Kiev or — in the great days of the Varangian Guard — even to Constantinople, and find himself among compatriots. Scandinavian archeologists have discovered almost 250,000 Viking Age coins; minted as far afield as Tashkent, Byzantium, and Ireland, they suggest that east-west commerce thrived between the years 800 and 1050 and that the Northmen dominated it. Excavation of large Viking trading marts such as Birka in Sweden and Hedeby in what now is Germany confirms the vital mercantile role of the Norse.

Not surprisingly, ocean trade still provides the economic lifeline of Scandinavia. For example, Norway's merchant fleet is the fourth largest in the world, and foreign trade per capita exceeds that of any other European country. In other respects, the modern scene bears a haunting resemblance to the distant past. Life along the fjords still adapts to the interplay of land and water. On the coasts farmers fish and fishermen farm; many work their own boats, most work their own land. Farms are small — only 10 percent exceed 20 acres. Family ties continue to be of prime importance.

Three sources illuminate the Viking Age and its historical background. Archeology reveals the actual articles and equipment of everyday living. Comments left by those who encountered Vikings at home or abroad acquaint us with their appearance and usages. Finally, the sagas — most of them composed in Iceland in the 13th century, some 200 or 300 years after the events they portray — provide sweeping histories of entire nations, important families, and individual northern heroes.

And, in the end, it is these heroes who loom largest in any study of the Viking Age. Wholly in love with life and half in love with death — poets, princes, and pirates — they dominate the era: Egil Skallagrimsson, whose verse mesmerized monarchs; Hrolf the Ganger, who won Normandy; Eric Bloodax, who ruled in York; Svein Forkbeard and Harald Hardraada and Leif the Lucky, Harald Bluetooth and Olaf the Stout — all that gallant, greedy, bloodstained band who shaped "a sword age, a wind age, a wolf age."

DAWN OF THE VIKING

arly sources cast only a fitful light on life in Scandinavia before the sudden eruption of the Viking Age. In his treatise *Germania*, written in the first century, Tacitus mentioned a people called the *Suiones* — doubtless forebears of the Swedes — well-armed, acquisitive, skilled in sailing curious ships "with a prow at each end." Five centuries later the Goth Jordanes reported on the ferocity of the inhabitants of Scandinavia, and on their extraordinary stature. Archeological finds have contributed a complementary picture of a comparatively primitive society based on agriculture, hunting, and fishing.

Geography — the fjords of Norway, Sweden's network of streams and lakes, Denmark's 500 islands — had early turned the Scandinavians seaward. From the Bronze Age on, they pioneered in the construction of swift, strong vessels. An affinity for ships, in fact, marks every phase of Scandinavian history.

Burials, our chief source of archeological information, followed a mixed pattern of cremations and inhumations, but nearly always included weapons, household utensils, and food. A great man or lady merited a fully fitted ship as a sepulcher; slaughtered horses, hounds, and slaves went along on that final voyage into the dark eternity of the burial mound. Lesser men were interred with boats. Those of no resources often had their graves covered by stones arranged in the outline of a boat.

From about A.D. 400 until the close of the sixth century, Europe was racked by what historians term the Great Migration Age. Moving generally from east to west, entire peoples — among them Huns, Goths, and Vandals — surged across the continent seizing territory by force of arms; in settling it, they dislocated the former populations which, in their turn, swelled the vast human tidal waves that ebbed and flowed in quest of land.

Although Angles and Jutes from Denmark did sweep into Britain, Scandinavia seems to have remained relatively stable during the Migration Age. Indeed, grave finds and buried hoards of gold and silver indicate that — while turmoil reigned in the south — Europe's northern reaches enjoyed a considerable degree of security and prosperity. One Swedish cache, discovered at Tureholm, contained more than 26 pounds of gold; another yielded some 15 pounds.

Throughout both the Migration Age and the succeeding Viking Age, the basic economic unit of Scandinavia was the family farm. Each farm aimed to be as self-sufficient as possible, and each family was a tightly knit labor force. The free peasant, the *karl* or *bondi*, had to master myriad skills. An ancient poem records the tasks of the good farmer who

> *Tamed the oxen and tempered plowshares,*
> *Timbered houses, and barns for the hay,*
> *Fashioned carts, and followed the plow.*

A wife sometimes joined her husband in the fields, but her primary responsibility was to provide daily necessities. She cooked and served meals, spun thread, wove cloth, made and washed garments, cleaned the dwelling,

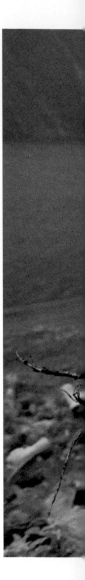

AGE

Laden with turnips—among the few vegetables grown in
Norway—Bjørn Skår pauses to listen to a call from his father. As
a younger son unlikely to take over the farm, Bjørn might
in time have gone viking had he lived a thousand years ago.

and milked the cows. The bunch of keys jangling at her waist signified her authority in such domestic activities.

At an early age, boys began to assist their father, and girls their mother.

One or more slaves, called *thralls*, performed the most obnoxious chores such as carrying faggots, cutting peat, tending swine, and spreading dung on the fields. Both before and during the Viking Age, slavery was commonplace in the North. Writing in the 11th century, the historian Adam of Bremen noted of Danish pirates that "they have no faith in one another, and as soon as one of them catches another, he mercilessly sells him into slavery either to one of his fellows or to a barbarian."

The average family inhabited a one-story, one- or two-room, rectangular house, with adjacent quarters for livestock. Benches banked the interior walls of the house, and a long hearth in the center provided light, warmth, and cooking facilities.

A typical day in sowing time—mid-April—began before daylight. Rising from the benches, which served for sleeping as well as sitting space, each member of the family trooped forth to his labors. In those northern latitudes, the farmer had a growing season of less than five months in which to provide the oats and barley that would sustain the household through the bleak winter. So first light found him and his sons already at work with plow and spade.

Indoors, his wife supervised the daughters at their chores. The women served the first meal of the day toward midmorning. The farmer took his place at the center of the table, sitting in a "high seat"; the rest of the family ranged themselves along the benches. Narrow tables held the food—typically porridge and buttermilk, eaten out of wooden bowls with wooden spoons, and either fish or dried mutton.

A short rest followed, then everyone resumed work until dark. After the second and last meal of the day—different from the first only in that the diners drank ale in great quantities—the wife would comb her husband's hair, help him disrobe, and cover him with an eiderdown as he retired on the bench.

Once he had finished planting, a man was likely to look toward the sea. With his neighbors he would sail off in the dragon ship of a local chieftain for a pleasant summer of pillage somewhere to the south. Until his return for the fall harvest, his wife controlled the affairs of the household. One grateful Swedish Viking even raised a runestone to the wife who acted as his surrogate: "No better mistress will come to Hassmyra, to look after the farm."

Literacy was much respected in the North, and recent evidence suggests that it was more prevalent than hitherto suspected. Runic characters—derived from the Roman and probably the Greek alphabets—first appear in Scandinavia about A.D. 200. Individual letters consist of straight strokes and combinations thereof clearly designed for carving on hard surfaces. Many early inscriptions found on weapons seem to represent the names bestowed upon them by their owners. This practice persisted throughout the age, and we know of Viking swords called *Gramr* (Fierce) and *Fótbítr* (Leg-biter).

Excavations in the old section of the Norwegian city of Bergen have brought to light some 500 inscriptions. Most are on small sticks, specially designed for runic messages, called *runakefli*. Although these finds date from two to three centuries after the Viking Age, they indicate the widespread use of runes at all levels of society. Some of the inscriptions have a startlingly familiar ring: "Kiss me, my darling" . . . "Ingebjørg loved me in Stavanger." And one, apparently passed into an ale shop by an irate wife to her inebriated husband, states: "Gyda says that you are to go home."

Investigators so far have found no townsites in Scandinavia antedating A.D. 800. Such petty kingdoms as did exist shifted borders with each skirmish, marriage, or new accession to the throne. Until almost the end of the Viking Age, the kings and carls *(jarls)* of the North reigned in glorified farmsteads, and the chief entertainment of the courts — particularly through the long gloom of winter — centered upon nightly drinking bouts.

Scandinavian royalty apparently possessed an almost limitless capacity for mead, a kind of honeyed ale, as well as a chilling propensity for finding death in the dregs of a drinking horn. The sagas inform us that an early Swedish king, Fjolnir, capped a night of festivity by stumbling drunkenly into a vat of mead wherein he drowned. A chronicle relates that a successor, Athils, perished after toasting the death of an enemy "with immoderate joviality." Following a long stint at the drinking bench, Sveigdir gave tipsy chase to a dwarf and was never seen again. Gudrod, who had forcibly captured and wed an unwilling princess, was skewered while inebriated by an agent of the unblushing bride.

One of these kings, Athils, lies in a huge mound at Gamla (Old) Uppsala, the royal seat of pagan Sweden. Two other sixth-century monarchs sleep in equally imposing man-made hills beside him, and many smaller barrows arc toward the horizon. I visited Gamla Uppsala after a snowfall, and children were slamming down the slopes of the mounds on red and yellow sleds. Yet for me there was no gaiety to the scene; the mounds are too high, too blunt, too funereal to support joy. Kings once burned here, and the smoke of the pyres seems to linger on the air. Neither snow nor frolicking children can soften the stark, heathen grandeur of these tombs.

From the royal mortuary, I crossed a road into the grove surrounding Old Uppsala Church, remnant of a 12th-century cathedral built upon the ruins of a pagan shrine. Adam of Bremen had described the original edifice as "entirely covered in gold."

Every nine years, Adam related, the whole nation flocked to a special festival at Uppsala. "Of every living thing that is male, they offer nine heads, with the blood of which it is customary to placate gods of this sort. The bodies they hang in the sacred grove that adjoins the temple. Now this grove is so sacred in the eyes of the heathen that each and every tree in it is believed divine because of the death or putrefaction of the victims. Even dogs and horses hang there with men."

Strolling among the trees, I glanced up, half-expecting to see the same grisly fruit silhouetted against the sky. But the Viking gods died long ago: grim,

*N*inth-century Gokstad ship — under sail, above, and fitted
with 32 oars, below — survives as a classic example of the swift
Viking warships used in coastal raids. It measures $76\frac{1}{2}$ feet in
length, and has a flexible oak frame and a strong keel.

*S*lower but more seaworthy, the Roskilde knarr, or deep-sea
trader, could carry livestock or a large cargo of other merchandise, and
had a crew of 15 to 20 men. Broad, deep, and 54 feet long,
the sturdy vessel plied the oceans almost exclusively under sail.

one-eyed Odin, deity of wisdom and war, the patron of kings and poets; bluff, mighty Thor, the storm god whose hammer pounded out thunderbolts; Frey, the god of fertility and increase, "who gives mankind peace and sensuous pleasures."

The ancient religion of the North boasted little theology and no promise of salvation. There was immortality of sorts—the more enjoyable for those of high station and for warriors. If you died fighting, the warrior-maids called Valkyries would escort you to Valhalla to fight all day and banquet all night until the distant time when the gods themselves—because in that fatalistic faith even the gods were doomed—fell in battle before the powers of darkness.

A saga informs us of a promise by Odin that everyone arriving in the realms of the dead would find all the objects burned with him on his pyre, as well as any treasure that he had buried during his lifetime. As a result, the funerals of chieftains and kings were pageants of pagan splendor. The anonymous author of the Old English epic *Beowulf* described such an occasion:

> *His dearest retainers carried the beloved*
> *Danish leader to the sea's edge. . . .*
> *Rime-crusted and eager to sail,*
> *A royal vessel with curved prow lay in harbor.*
> *They set down their dear king amidships, close by the mast.*
> *A mass of treasure was brought there from distant parts.*
> *No ship, they say, was ever so well equipped*
> *With swords, corselets, weapons, and armor.*
> *On the king's breast rested a heap of jewels. . . .*
> *High overhead they set his golden standard.*

The sagas offer this account of the burial of a ninth-century Norwegian king, Halvdan the Black: "There had been excellent seasons during his rule; and people were so affected by his death that when they learned of his demise and that his body was being taken to Hringaríki in order to be interred there, men of influence from Raumaríki, Westfold, and Heithmork came and prayed, all of them, to take the body with them to be buried in their lands; for it was thought that he who got possession of it could expect good seasons. They reached an agreement in this wise, that the body was assigned to four places: The head was laid in a mound at Stein in Hringaríki, but each of the others carried away their share and interred them in burial mounds in their homelands."

Superstition reigned everywhere in the pagan North. Of all the desirable qualities a man might possess, luck ranked first—far above skill or intelligence or virtue. Certain individuals won wide renown for woman-luck or weapon-luck. And when a Norseman decided to go viking for a summer, he sought a chief famed for his victory-luck.

Christian priests, on the other hand, were notorious for a lack of weather-luck, and no skipper willingly transported one of them on his ship. Until the general conversion of Scandinavia, crews hurled many a priestly passenger screaming into the sea at first sight of an ominous cloud on the horizon.

The Vikings balanced their blood-reeking religion and murky superstitions with a passion for poetry. The art of the *skalds*, or court poets, followed a complex, rigid formula that featured alliteration, internal rhyme, and the elaborate metaphors called kennings. "Hawkfell," for example, formed a kenning for "hand," since thereon perched one's hunting falcon; a battle might be "the reddening of spears" or "the Valkyries' magic song"; blood became "wound-dew," and to slay enemies was "to feed the ravens" or "sate the eagles."

Poets of the Viking Age prospered as never before and never since, for verse alone could memorialize the deeds of great men. No self-respecting king or jarl would venture into battle without a complement of skalds behind his shield-wall. King Harald Hardraada of Norway, himself no mean poet, cannily assured eternal fame by playing host to dozens, mostly Icelanders; he took three on his ill-fated final journey to England. The poets traded their verse unashamedly for gold; the greatest of them, Egil Skallagrimsson, in a stately lament for his friend and patron, Jarl Arinbjørn, unblushingly wondered who would now

> *Fill high hawkfell of my hand*
> *With skald's reward for skilled word?*

Poetry, if well enough crafted, could even forestall the wrath of kings. One bizarre occasion found the same Egil literally composing for his life. After falling into the hands of his sworn foe Eric Bloodax, who reigned briefly over the Viking Kingdom of York in England, Egil fashioned a poem overnight. As the king brooded on his high seat the next morning, the skald recited 20 dazzling stanzas in praise of his royal captor. With an eye wisely cocked to immortality rather than mere vengeance, Eric spared his blood enemy. Rich testimony to the cleverness of Egil and the vanity of Eric, the poem lives still and bears the fitting title *Head Ransom.*

If a skald's words could buy life, so could they also mock death. In the 11th-century battle of Stiklarstadir, Norwegian King Olaf Haraldsson's skald Thormod jerked an enemy arrow from his chest, carefully examined the tip, and proclaimed: "Well has the king fed us; I still have fat around the roots of my heart." Whereupon he fell dead.

Pursued by thoughts of ringing poetry and bloody sacrifice, I left the grove of the old gods. I capped my stay at Gamla Uppsala with a visit to the inn of Odinsborg—Odin's Castle. From a window in the dining room, I looked out across the sinister barrows and silently toasted Athils with a specialty of the house: a horn of foaming mead.

Later, I discussed the dawn of the Viking Age with a Scandinavian archeologist. Why, after the raid at Lindisfarne, did Norsemen suddenly appear virtually everywhere in Europe?

"The pre-Viking North was a self-contained society," he told me. "Swedes, Norwegians, and Danes spoke a common language, shared a common culture, and knew relatively little of the world outside Scandinavia. Just preceding the Viking Age, we find evidence of a marked population explosion. The number of burials multiplies and place names increase.

"But the land couldn't support more people. So they took to their ships — the finest in the world at that time and for centuries to come — and solved the problem by raiding the richer lands to the south and trading for foreign goods on a grand scale. But remember, the trading was always more important to the home economy than the raiding."

In furtherance of this vital commerce, northern merchants of early Viking times established a series of trade centers. The remains of one lie in the German state of Schleswig-Holstein, which abuts on southern Denmark and, in Viking days, was Danish territory. From the present-day city of Schleswig, I peered across the Schlei inlet and wondered how many vessels had once knifed through these slate waters to moor before the booths of the Viking town — Hedeby — that had stood across the way. I could see the flat, 60-acre townsite protected by an earthern rampart on three sides; the fourth opened onto the Schlei, an intruding finger of the Baltic Sea.

Along with Birka in Sweden, Hedeby had served as a kind of central mart for Scandinavia from the 9th to the 11th centuries. Norse merchants had played host to Slavs, Franks, Saxons, Celts, and even Arabs who converged on the town to barter silver for slaves, silks for furs, wine for swords. Resident craftsmen had supplied ornaments carved from bone, along with leatherware, cloth, jewelry, and pottery.

Al-Tartushi, a traveler from Moorish Córdoba, visited Hedeby about 950 at the zenith of its prosperity. He found "a large town at the very far end of the world ocean. It has freshwater wells within the city. Its people worship Sirius except a few who are Christians and have a church there. . . . A feast is held to honor their deity and to eat and drink. Any man who slaughters a sacrificial animal — whether it is an ox, ram, goat, or pig — fastens it up on poles outside his house to show that he has made his sacrifice in honor of the god. The town is poorly provided with property or treasure. The inhabitants' principal food is fish, which is plentiful. The people often throw a newborn child into the sea rather than maintain it. Furthermore women have the right to claim a divorce; they do this themselves whenever they wish."

The merriment of the citizens depressed him. "I have never heard such horrible singing . . . it is like a growl coming out of their throats, like the barking of dogs only still more brutish."

Dr. Kurt Schietzel of the Schleswig-Holstein National Museum for Pre- and Early History directs the monumental project of excavating Hedeby. As he does so, he is also revolutionizing archeology.

During my first visit to Hedeby in 1969, I joined Dr. Schietzel on the townsite. "When I came here seven years ago," he told me, "we were excavating in the conventional fashion. We dug through the summer, filled in for the winter, then went back to work the following summer. Hobbled by that technique, archeologists had dug up only six percent of the site since 1902. Obviously I had to speed things up."

Dr. Schietzel, who is young and inventive — and so devoted to his job that

he has taken only one holiday since he started — first constructed a huge, mobile tent that runs on rails. Working inside, his year-round labor force stripped off the accumulated debris of Hedeby in carefully sifted strata, never more than six inches. "When we reach bottom, we advance the tent and start anew," he said. "A draftsman sketches each level in exact detail, and we catalogue every object as to type, level, and location.

"It's an assembly line of sorts. But our problem here is unprecedented in archeology: We find too much. Often we uncover 500 to 600 significant objects a day. No one could handle such a flood with the old methods, so we've had to devise new ones."

Back in his laboratory, he led me into a large freezing-locker, another of his innovations: Here he stores perishable items found on the site until they can be examined at leisure by experts and suitably conserved. He showed me frozen coils of rope, leather shoes, textiles, and wood, all faintly blanched with frost. "By the end of this year," he announced as we shivered in the 0° F. vault, "we will have collected 300,000 pieces from Hedeby as well as more than 500,000 selected bones. We will then stop digging for several years and publish the results of our work."

In 1972 I visited Hedeby again and found Dr. Schietzel, aided by a far-flung network of scholars, pursuing just that course. In order to expedite publication of the spectacular results of his dig, Dr. Schietzel has made his finds available to specialists from as far afield as France and Czechoslovakia.

Blacksmith forges a heavy knife. The smith held a prestigious and prosperous place in Norse society, and worked with a considerable range of tools. One tenth-century grave yielded—clockwise from lower left—a ladle (side and bottom views), a planishing hammer (side, top, and end views), tongs, shears, a file, chisels, and heavy hammerheads.

"Our work," he told me, "shows that Hedeby expanded dramatically early in the ninth century—about the beginning of the Viking Age—maintained a position of salient importance in trade for perhaps 50 to 100 years, and then, in the tenth century, gradually declined. In its prime, it functioned as a kind of Hudson's Bay Company station. I draw the parallel because Hedeby stood in a totally undeveloped area. In fact, it is unique in the Viking world; of all the trading centers discovered, Hedeby alone has no hinterland. It existed only to enable the people of this region to acquire the civilized trade goods they craved. The permanent population, anywhere from several hundreds to a maximum of a thousand, was swelled to double by summer arrivals. From May to September, the local farmers and visiting merchants struck their bargains and then went their ways."

The merchants, of course, traveled by ship. And the superb ships of the North are the key to the entire Viking achievement. Their seaworthiness and swiftness enabled Norse mariners to range the world at will.

Amazingly, some of these magnificent vessels have survived the centuries. Arne Emil Christensen, Jr., a curator of the University Museum of National Antiquities in Oslo and technical consultant for this book, accompanied me on my first visit to Norway's famed Viking Ship Hall. The vaulted silence of the hall framed a magnificent vista. There, as we entered, the serpent prow of the Oseberg ship sailed inexorably out of the past. A sublime work of art, richly decorated, beautifully proportioned, it apparently served as a ceremonial yacht for a queen. The ship had seen almost 50 years of use before being buried beside the Oslo Fjord in the middle of the ninth century.

"Almost certainly this was the type of vessel that raided Lindisfarne in 793," said Mr. Christensen. "It's quite beautiful, but has serious weaknesses. The freeboard measures a scant foot, making it extremely vulnerable to swamping. And the towering stem and stern, each 15 feet tall, would have caught the wind and made it unstable."

We passed on to the less ornate Gokstad ship, found north of Sandefjord in 1880. "Now this was built a generation or two after the Oseberg," Mr. Christensen said. "The shipwright has given the hull a more efficient shape, improved the mast step, and added two feet of freeboard. Apart from the crossbeams, there isn't a single straight piece of wood in this ship. All the strakes are of solid oak, hewed from naturally curved planks, and the grain runs with the curve. The ribs and planking below the waterline are lashed together with spruce roots, giving the ship tremendous flexibility in heavy seas.

"With all the resources of modern technology, you could not construct a more seaworthy ship of this type. It's a classic."

In 1893 a Norwegian crew sailed an exact copy of the Gokstad ship across

Danish Boy Scouts and their leaders sail replicas they constructed

of dragon-prowed Viking vessels: Sebbe Als (right)

and Imme Gram. Like the builders of the original

longships that traversed such rugged European coasts

as Spain's Cabo Finisterre (above), the scouts lashed

rather than nailed strakes and ribs for greater flexibility.

the Atlantic. They experienced no difficulty en route. In fact, the captain later reported enthusiastically that "we often had the pleasure of darting through the water at speeds of 10, and sometimes even 11, knots. This in spite of a primitive and relatively small rigging!"

Each of the reconstructed ships had served as a sepulcher — Gokstad for a chieftain, Oseberg for a lady of high estate. When archeologists dug up the Oseberg ship in 1904, they found aboard it the bodies of two women — one old and arthritic, the other young and healthy. Scholars believe that the younger woman was sacrificed to accompany her mistress on the death voyage.

I toured the rich trove of grave goods — wood carvings of unbelievable complexity, collapsible tents and beds for shipboard use, gilded ornaments, textiles, and two trim small boats found in the Gokstad barrow.

"You know," Mr. Christensen told me, "the old Norse were absolutely obsessed by ships. They regarded them much as the British 19th-century aristocracy regarded horses. Essentially, the Gokstad and Oseberg vessels are pieces of sculpture. The shipwrights worked without plans. They shaped the shell with hand and eye, then fitted the ribs to the planking."

Ship aesthetics did indeed dominate many a Viking mind. A saga relates how one master builder, Thorberg Skafhogg, took an ax to the legendary *Long Serpent* constructed for King Olaf Tryggvason of Norway because he found its lines inelegant. Told to repair the scars or lose his head, he seized the opportunity to reshape the vessel into what became his masterpiece.

The Viking art of boat building has survived — but barely — to our own day. In the fjords of West Norway, a few men still make lithe and handsome craft in the old fashion. I found one in the little village of Lysekloster that hugs the edge of the Lyse Fjord, an hour's drive from Bergen.

"It's always sad for me to visit him," a Norwegian friend had told me. "I think it will be sad for you, too. Twenty years ago 15 such boat builders worked in this district. Now only he remains alive."

Arriving in Lysekloster, I picked my way down a steep slope to the edge of the fjord where a sprawling wooden workshop bore the sign *A. Søvik, Båtbygger*. The crystal waters of the fjord slapped at a small wharf beside the barnlike building. Landward, forested hills soared high and green.

Mr. Søvik, compact, gray-haired, well into his sixties, led me into his workshop where accumulated wood shavings curled shoulder-high against the walls. The air was redolent of pine, and a partially completed boat lay on stocks in the center of the room.　　　　　　　　　　　　*(Continued on page 34)*

Holy relics in his arms, a monk of Lindisfarne flees from marauding Norwegians. Their

...esecration of the monastery in 793 heralded more than 250 years of Viking terror.

Embracing earth and sky, a tree symbolizes the realms of creation in Norse religion. Supreme among the gods stood Odin, who conferred victory or defeat in battle. His eight-legged horse, carved on a picture stone (opposite, bottom), carried slain warriors to feast in Valhalla, where his

handmaidens, the Valkyries, served them. Red-bearded Thor, lord of the sky and thunder, reigned as popular champion of the common man. Single-handed he struggled with the World Serpent in the ocean depths. Frey, chief god of fertility, presided over agriculture, rain, and sunshine.

Serpent, gold, Norway
1 1/4 TIMES ACTUAL SIZE

Thor, bronze, Iceland
3/4 ACTUAL SIZE

Frey, bronze, Sweden
3/4 ACTUAL SIZE

Valkyrie, silver, Sweden
2 TIMES ACTUAL SIZE

Odin's horse Sleipnir, Sweden

"It's a good way from being finished," Mr. Søvik said. "A few weeks' more work. It's for a fisherman here in the fjord."

The vessel was taking shape as a sister to the small boats dug up with the Gokstad ship, even to the incised parallel lines that decorated every plank. The strakes overlapped, and—just as in the recovered Viking vessels—rivets fastened them together.

"Who builds boats like these nowadays?" Mr. Søvik asked with gentle irony. "Just some old men with no ability for anything else."

He traced a strake with a finger.

"I use only naturally curved wood. I find the timber I need while walking through the forest. You mark this tree as properly bent, or that as having an ideal fork for a stem or stern. Then when you need them, you fell them."

Mr. Søvik showed me his tools; all could have come from a Viking burial mound. "They're not commercially available, of course, so I must have them forged," he said.

Straddling a plank, he swung an ax in graceful, almost metronomic strokes, demonstrating how he hewed the wood into its final, impeccably smooth shape. When he finished, he was panting.

"Pardon me," he said. "But I've had several heart attacks. I can't work at full speed anymore."

In the Viking tradition, he uses no plans, relying on hand and eye to shape the exquisite shell of the boat. And his unit of measurement is the all-but-forgotten *alen* (approximately 21 inches) employed by old Norse shipwrights.

"I learned how to make boats from my father, and he from his father. My family transmitted the techniques from generation to generation. But now I have no sons. And I can find no apprentice. Young men today, with their advanced educations, take no satisfaction in building old-fashioned boats."

Because I couldn't think of anything else to say, I motioned awkwardly to the tools and stacked planks and asked, "What will happen to all of this when you retire?"

He smiled wryly. "After me—plastic."

So I left him, a maritime sculptor, an artist of the end time, shaping his archaic symmetries in the solitary shop beside the Lyse Fjord. With him and his kind would die an art that began in the Bronze Age—an art that had fathered the sleek sea-steeds and wave-plungers that first conquered the western ocean. I trudged up the slope with the rueful knowledge that my friend had been right about the sadness.

TRADERS: THE BALTIC

orne on their swift ships, driven by a lust for gold and glory, the Scandinavians struck out in force in the ninth century. Danes and Norwegians generally steered their longships down through the North Sea toward the inviting and ill-defended coasts of Britain, Ireland, and continental Europe. The Swedes thrust across the Baltic into the vast birch forests and steppes of Russia. Skimming rivers and lakes, making difficult portages whenever necessary, they pressed ever southward, pursuing the Volga and the Dnieper toward the wondrous marts of Baghdad and Byzantium. As they advanced, they established strongholds at key points: Smolensk, Rostov, Chernigov. With them went cargoes of furs, honey, amber, wax, and—most important—fair slaves to be traded for the silks and silver of the Orient. So heavy was the traffic that a hundred thousand silver coins from such cities as Samarkand and Tashkent have come to light in Swedish hoards.

Any account of the Viking penetration of Russia soon runs afoul of one of the most acrimonious controversies ever to sunder scholarly ranks—the "Varangian problem." Throughout eastern Europe, the word Varangian—perhaps from Old Slavic *varjag* (itinerant merchants) or Old Norse *váraring* (pledged men or confederates)—referred to Northmen. Russians called the Baltic the Varangian Sea; the trading route between Scandinavia and the Black Sea became known as the Varangian Way.

On one side of the Varangian problem, the Normanist school—almost exclusively Westerners—maintains that Swedish Vikings not only dominated Russia in the ninth and tenth centuries but actually founded the Russian state. The anti-Normanists—almost exclusively Russians—assert that, at best, those Vikings who left their traces along the Varangian Way served as mercenaries in Slavic hire. The disagreement is total: Words and traditions and graves and artifacts declared to be Scandinavian by the Normanists are labeled Slavic by the anti-Normanists.

The two schools snipe irritably at each other's findings, but scholars from both camps would agree that Swedish Vikings *did* appear in Russia in the ninth century. They would also agree that the newcomers used Novgorod, called Holmgård by the Northmen, as a major trading base, and that the first rulers of Kiev—one of the most powerful states of 11th-century Europe and the nucleus of modern Russia—were Scandinavians.

The evidence indicates that the energetic Swedes attained supremacy over the native populations, and in Novgorod their leaders ruled as princes. Contemporary documents refer to these merchant-colonists as the *Rus*, possibly a corruption of the Finnish word for Sweden, *Ruotsi*, from *rodr*, or Rowing Way. In any case, they eventually gave their name to the entire country: Russia.

The Vikings apparently maintained their suzerainty and separate identity in Novgorod until about the year 1020. Thereafter they were swiftly assimilated into the Slavic population. A few Scandinavian given names lingered on in corrupted forms until the 15th century. Examination of chronicles and records

TO BYZANTIUM

Skier nears the finish of a 15-mile race in the Småland Highlands of Sweden. Scandinavian skill at cross-country skiing goes back more than a thousand years.

of medieval Novgorod has revealed such examples as Ivor (Ivarr), Uleb (Olaf), Aldan (Halfdan), and Jakun (Hakon). Not surprisingly, the Norse names occurred with far greater frequency among the aristocrats than elsewhere on the social scale.

Sailing out of Novgorod, the Rus not only learned the trade route to Constantinople but, by 839, also seem to have drawn the notice of the imperial court. In that year a Byzantine legation arrived before the Frankish emperor, Louis the Pious, in Ingleheim. With them these emissaries brought some Rus envoys who had been sent to Constantinople; tribal wars along the rivers had prevented their return, and the Byzantine emperor requested that Louis repatriate them by way of his realm. Interrogation showed that the Rus were in fact Swedish. Louis, whose shores had often been harassed by Northmen, promptly ordered them held for further investigation—with what result the account fails to report.

Arab merchants and diplomats frequently encountered the Rus on Russian rivers. "They sail their ships," wrote the geographer Ibn Rustah, "to ravage the Slavs, and bring back captives whom they sell to the Khazars and Bulgars. They have no cultivated fields but depend for their supplies on what they can obtain from the Slavic land. When a son is born the father will go up to the newborn baby, sword in hand; throwing it down, he says, 'I shall not leave you any property: you have only what you can provide with this weapon!'"

An Arab diplomat, Ibn Fadlan, met the Rus on the Volga: "Never had I seen people of more perfect physique; they are tall as date palms, blond and ruddy. They wear neither coat nor mantle, but each man carries a cape which covers one half of his body, leaving one hand free. Their swords are Frankish in pattern, broad, flat, and fluted."

The fastidious Arab went on to brand the Rus "the filthiest of God's creatures." In the light of this comment, one can only shudder at the standards of hygiene that must have prevailed in Anglo-Saxon England. For there, John of Wallingford excoriated Danish Vikings for excessive cleanliness. "They still had from their native land," he noted, "the custom of combing the hair daily and on the Sabbath to bathe, often indeed to change clothing . . . whence did they . . . seduce chaste matrons."

In 922, Ibn Fadlan witnessed the ship burial of a Rus chief beside the Volga. His description is one of the most remarkable documents of the Viking Age. At the death of the chief, wrote the Arab, "they laid him in his grave and roofed it over for ten days while they cut out and made ready his clothes. What they do is this: for a poor man they make a small boat, place him in it and then burn it; but if he is rich, they gather together his wealth and divide it into three—one part for his family, one part to provide clothes for him and a third part for *nabidh* [a fermented drink], which they drink on the day that the slave woman is killed and burned together with her master. They stupefy themselves by drinking this *nabidh* night and day; sometimes one of them dies cup in hand. When the man of whom I have spoken died, his girl slaves were asked, 'Who will die with him?' One answered 'I.' ... Two female slaves were appointed to guard her wherever she went so that they even washed her feet with their own hands. Then they began to get things ready for the dead man; to cut out his clothes and do all that should be done, but the slave drank and sang every day happily and joyfully.

"When the day came that the dead man should be burned together with his slave, I went to the river where the ship lay. It had been hauled up on land and supported by four posts of birch and other wood. Around it was arranged what looked like a large pile of wood. The ship was then drawn up and placed on the wood. People began to go to and fro and spoke words which I did not understand, but the corpse still lay in the grave from which they had not yet taken it. They then brought a bier which was placed in the ship; they covered it with Byzantine brocaded tapestries and with cushions of Byzantine brocade.

"Then an old woman, whom they call the Angel of Death, came and spread these hangings on the bier. She is in charge of embalming the dead man and preparing him and it is she who kills the girl. The one I saw was a strongly-built and grim figure."

The corpse was removed from the grave and clothed in "trousers, boots and tunic, and a brocade mantle with gold buttons on it. They placed a cap made of brocade and sable on his head. They carried him into a tent which stood on the ship, and laid him on the tapestry and propped him up with the cushions. Then they brought *nabidh*, fruit and sweet-smelling herbs and laid these beside him. Next they brought bread, meat and onions and threw these beside him. Next they took two horses which they caused to run until they were sweating, after which they cut them in pieces with a sword and threw their flesh into the ship. Then they brought two cows, which they also cut into pieces, and threw them in."

After a brief ritual, the slave girl was led to the ship. "She then took off two armbands which she had on and gave them to the old woman who was called the Angel of Death. ... Then came men who had shields and staves, and gave her a beaker of *nabidh*. She sang over it and drained it. The interpreter said to me, 'She now takes farewell of her friends.' Then she was given another beaker. She took this and sang for a long time, but the old woman warned her that she should drink quickly and go into the tent where her master lay. When I looked at her, she seemed bemused, she wanted to go into the tent but [seemed unable to control herself] ... then the old woman took her hand and made her enter the tent and went in with her. The men began to beat with their staves on the shields so that her shrieks should not be heard and the other girls should not be frightened and thus not seek death with their masters. ...

"They laid her by the side of her dead master, then two took her legs, two took her hands, and the old woman who is called the Angel of Death put a rope round her neck, with the ends in opposite directions, and gave it to two men to pull; then she came with a dagger with a broad blade and began to thrust it time and again between the girl's ribs, while the two men choked her with the rope so that she died.

"Then came one who was nearest related to the dead man. He took a piece

of wood and fired it. Then he went backwards towards the ship with his face towards the people and held the torch in one hand; his other hand was on his backside. He was naked. Thus the wood which lay under the ship was fired after they had laid the slave woman whom they had killed by the side of her master. Then people came with wood and branches—everyone had a piece of burning wood. They threw it on the wood which lay under the ship so that the fire took hold of the pyre, then of the ship, then of the tent and of the man and of the girl and of all that was in the ship. A powerful, fearful wind began to blow so that the flames became fiercer and more intense. . . . An hour had not passed before the ship, the wood, the girl, and her master were nothing but cinders and ashes.''

I have seen archeologists' evidence of ship burials from Russia to the Isle of Man, from the Oslo Fjord to Brittany. One can only wonder how many thousands of times during the Viking Age this savage scene unfolded.

Pushing southward down the Volga, the Rus debouched into the Caspian

Gift to the gods—a black grouse—takes wing from under an oak tree on an island in the Dnieper. Scandinavian merchants, journeying from Kiev to Constantinople, customarily paused midway to express gratitude for safe passage of a section of river filled with peril: seething rapids and nomadic bands of robbers.

Sea. This they did in strength for the first time in about 912, by striking a bargain with the Khagan of the Khazars, a curious people that controlled much of southeastern Russia including the mouth of the Volga and a portion of Transcaucasia. Although a Turkic race, the Khazars, or at least the ruling classes, had converted to Judaism sometime around 740. Their empire endured until the late tenth century, and the names of their kings—Obediah, Aaron, David, Joseph—echo down the centuries like a drum roll from the Old Testament.

Once the Vikings had agreed to divide their booty with the Khazars, they sailed into the Caspian. There they fell without mercy upon the populations of Azerbaijan and northern Persia. The account of the Moslem chronicler rings with anguish:

"The ar-Rus shed blood, ravished women and children, plundered . . . destroyed and burned. . . . Then the people prepared themselves for war . . . but the ar-Rus attacked them and thousands of Muslims were killed or drowned."

In one of their forays the Northmen captured Baku. The present-day city, of course, ranks as an important oil producer in the U.S.S.R., but even a thousand years ago Baku fueled the war machines of Byzantium and even of faraway Moorish Spain. For everywhere in that petroleum-saturated region lay pools of highly volatile naphtha, the basic ingredient for Greek fire, the napalm of medieval warfare.

The Islamic heritage of Baku, I discovered, has been all but obliterated by a modern metropolis of formidable drabness. Amid utilitarian structures of commerce and industry, a few minarets and mosques with old, pure Arab lines —visions of time past—quietly decay. Thousands of derricks tirelessly pumping crude oil line the horizon in all directions, even marching far out into the Caspian. Skeletal and black, they encompass the city like a burned-out forest. The smokestacks of oil refineries belch sooty clouds into the blue Asian sky, and a southeast wind, the *Gilavar*, gusts through the streets, carrying dust from the distant Kara Kum desert. In other seasons, the *Khazri*—named for the long-departed Khazars—blows from the north. Whenever the wind dies down, the air fills with a smell of hot oil.

If Baku is somewhat eerie now, it was no less so when the Vikings saw it. Not far from the city, a "fountain" of natural gas roars from the earth; in ancient times it burned brightly, and fire-venerating Parsees journeyed there from Persia and India to build a temple. Then as now, underground pressures produced sporadic eruptions of mud. Ponds of naphtha and lakes of asphalt dotted the landscape, and the earth shuddered with endless subterranean disturbances.

How the raiders from the north must have marveled as they approached this strange land of blazing fountains, flammable lakes, and undying winds!

But almost predictably, the Rus fell victims to a classic double cross when they steered back into the Volga. With Khazar complicity, vengeful Moslems attacked them and "the sword took the ar-Rus." Viking casualties, according to the Arabs, numbered some 30,000.

Doubtless this experience helps explain why the Dnieper became the principal Viking route through Russia. By 860, two Northmen named Askold and Dir had seized control of Kiev—a city situated on high ground that dominates the Dnieper 570 river-miles north of the Black Sea. In the same year, under their command, a Rus fleet emerged from the mouth of the Dnieper, sailed west, and boldly attacked Constantinople. This imperial capital every Viking knew simply as Miklagård, the Big City.

Although the attackers—200 ships strong—failed to take Miklagård, they sacked the suburbs and hinterland with unprecedented savagery. Preaching after the repulse of the Viking assault, the Patriarch Photius could quickly evoke the old horror in his congregation: "Do you remember this unbearable time when the barbarian ships came to our shores, breathing something wild, severe and destructive. . . . Do you remember when the terror and darkness had robbed your reason, and your ear could hear only the alarming news; the barbarians have penetrated the walls, the enemy is conquering the city! . . . You, who have captured many trophies from enemies out of Europe, Asia, and Levant, are now threatened by a spear held by a brutal, barbarian hand which would make a trophy of you!"

Why did Constantinople attract would-be conquerors, not only from Kiev but from every quarter of East and West alike? In an age of general squalor, it was a city of gold; while the capitals of the West counted populations of a few thousand, Constantinople boasted almost a million inhabitants. Emperors—their lives a splendid, ritualized pageant—represented an imperial continuity that reached back to Augustus Caesar.

When early in the fourth century the Roman Empire became too unwieldy for centralized control, Constantine the Great had divided it into two sectors by building an eastern capital. He chose a superb site where the Bosporus empties into the Sea of Marmara and only a mile of open water separates Europe from Asia. While the western empire soon fell into decline, the eastern—or

Byzantine—prospered; Constantine's city became the focal point of trade between Europe and Asia.

In the middle of the ninth century the imperial frontiers extended from Armenia to Sicily, and included Greece and parts of the Balkans and the Crimea. Gradually, Greek—long the *lingua franca* of the eastern Mediterranean—had supplanted Latin as the language of the court. But some of the old terminology lingered: The emperor was called Caesar, the empress was the Augusta. Citizens referred to themselves interchangeably as Greeks and Romans.

Behind the imposing Golden Gate that gave ceremonial access to Constantinople stood palaces of marble, and bazaars that overflowed with exotic merchants and wares from Europe, Asia, and Africa. Chariots raced in the hippodrome before hysterically cheering throngs; splendid mosaics adorned the churches and public buildings. Dominating the city was the huge and magnificent cathedral of Hagia Sophia, Holy Wisdom, built in the sixth century by Justinian. Until the construction of St. Peter's in Rome in the 16th century, it remained the largest and loveliest shrine in Christendom.

To bedazzle barbarian eyes further, the emperor occupied an ingenious mechanical throne designed to emphasize the might of Byzantium and the insignificance of foreign ambassadors. In 948 Liudprand of Cremona led an embassy to Constantinople where he was received by Emperor Constantine Porphyrogenitus. He left this account: "Before the emperor's seat stood a tree, made of bronze gilded over, whose branches were filled with birds, also made of gilded bronze, which uttered different cries. . . . The throne itself was so marvellously fashioned that at one moment it seemed a low structure, and at another it rose high into the air [perhaps by means of a large screw device]. It was of immense size and was guarded by lions, made either of bronze or of wood covered over with gold, who beat the ground with their tails and gave a dreadful roar with open mouth and quivering tongue. Leaning upon the shoulders of two eunuchs I was brought into the emperor's presence. At my approach the lions began to roar and the birds to cry out. . . . After I had three times made obeisance to the emperor with my face upon the ground, I lifted my head, and behold! the man whom just before I had seen sitting on a moderately elevated seat had now changed his raiment and was sitting on the level of the ceiling."

Such wonders and such opulence could not fail to kindle Viking greed, and in 907 the Rus arrived once more beneath the walls of Miklagård. This time they were led by Oleg, "Great Prince of the Rus." Oleg, ruler of Novgorod, had sallied down the Dnieper a few years before and seized Kiev, had slain his fellow Northmen Askold and Dir, and in effect had made that strategic city the capital of his realm.

Although Oleg's fleet failed to vanquish Miklagård, he did extract favorable treaty terms: Rus traders were guaranteed entry to the city's marts, and Byzantine authorities even agreed to provide suitable facilities for baths. The Kievan envoys subscribed to the terms thus: "We of the Rus nation: Karl, Ingjald, Farulf, Vermund, Hrollaf, Gunnar, Harald, Karni, Frithleif, Hroarr, Angantyr,

Throand, Leithulf, Fast, and Steinvith, are sent by Oleg, Great Prince of the Rus ... for the maintenance and proclamation of the long-standing amity which joins Greeks and Rus. ..." The list contains not a single Slavic name, and even Oleg derives from the Scandinavian Helgi.

Kiev, ancient stronghold of the Rus, is now the third largest city in the Soviet Union and capital of the fertile Ukraine. The oldest section of Kiev stands on a bluff above the west bank of the Dnieper. Trees line the pleasant, winding streets, and the towers of churches and monasteries — most of them inoperative by government decree — dominate the skyline.

Although Viking burials have come to light in Kiev, probably the most vivid relic of the Northmen's rule stands on a hill overlooking the Dnieper some 35 miles below the city. The site is called Vitichev, and when Academician B. A. Rybakov excavated it between 1956 and 1958, he found the remains of an 11th-century fortification — wooden walls filled with earth.

On a freezing November day, I bounced down the Dnieper in a small, swift hydrofoil. The wind tore at the open boat and both the driver and I crouched low behind the windshield. Below Kiev, the river offers a bleak vista. In all directions stretch the endless, monotonous, but incredibly fertile steppes that make the Ukraine the larder of the U.S.S.R.

Only a tiny wharf and shed on the west bank mark Vitichev. When we had tied up, I trudged to the top of a 235-foot hill, the dominant feature of the gray, empty landscape. There, on the summit, I wandered through Rybakov's dig. He had identified the foundation of a tower that apparently had served both for observation and signaling; he had also found charred wood and barrels that had contained tar; from the size of the fortified area, Soviet experts estimate that it housed a garrison of about a hundred.

The evidence was convincing that Vitichev had served as an outpost for Viking-ruled Kiev, and that the tar had fueled a beacon atop the tower — a common warning device among the Northmen — that alerted the city to impending raids. The name has an Old Norse root, *viti* (signal fire or beacon), and is mentioned both in Norse documents (as Vitaholm) and in Russian (as Vitichev).

Standing on the hill, I looked out across the slate-colored Dnieper — shallow, turbid, scarred with white sand bars — and I remembered the runic inscription on the 11th-century Alstad stone in Oslo's University Museum:

Engle raised this stone after Torald his son
Who found death in Vitaholm between Ustaholm and Gardar.

Ustaholm, based on the Russian word for mouth, *ust'e*, presumably refers to the point where the Trubëzh River flows into the Dnieper, about 30 miles south of Vitichev; Gardar — "place of towns" in Old Norse — probably meant the district of Kiev. In his book on imperial administration, the Byzantine emperor Constantine Porphyrogenitus pointed out that in the spring Rus vessels gathered at Vitichev before daring the cataracts leading to the Black Sea and the marts of Miklagård. Was it in such a springtime that Torald — with Byzantium almost in sight and his fortune assured — met his (Continued on page 52)

*S*wedish merchant measures a bolt of cloth offered in exchange
for his furs. The style of his trousers reflects Eastern influence. By the
tenth century, Northmen were trading with all the known world.

In snowy Hedeby, a trading center on Jutland's Baltic coast, merchants ar

...ttlers barter farm products, cloth, pottery, glass, weapons, and slaves.

New Hedeby, a reconstruction of the Viking town, rises in Denmark with
the help of Boy Scout volunteers. Sod covers one roof; bundles of thatch
will complete another. Hedeby flourished until 1049, when Harald Hardraada
burned it. Moss tints the protruding shapes of unfinished pots in a centuries-
old soapstone quarry in Norway (opposite, upper); the Vikings carved
cooking vessels from the soft, heat-retaining material. Amber, much prized for
jewelry in the Middle Ages, still washes up on North Sea beaches.

Reconstruction of a craftsman's home, its gable ends copied from Viking

tent frames, overlooks a roughhewn boardwalk in New Hedeby. At right,

a scout duplicating an old charcoal-making process feeds firewood

into a flaming pit before covering it for 24 hours. Under sure hands

(lower right), a section of decorative carving takes shape.

unlucky end? And did he and his boat and slave burn beside this timeless river?

Over glasses of tea that evening, I discussed the early history of Kiev with a member of the Institute of Archeology of the Academy of Sciences of the Ukraine. "To be sure," he said, "the Vikings loomed very large in this city from the 9th to the 11th centuries. It's notable that the early rulers of Kiev had Norse names, but the names of the later and probably the greatest princes, Vladimir and Yaroslav, were purely Slavic. I think what is true of the Vikings in Kiev is true of the Vikings everywhere: In the end, they assimilated into the local population, leaving no discernible mark on the culture.

"Vladimir, however, who came to power in 980, most certainly determined the future course of the Russian nation. There is a tradition that Vladimir—for political reasons—determined to replace paganism with one of the mono-theistic religions. He sent emissaries abroad to report on Judaism, Islam, the Roman Catholic Church, and the Orthodox Church. He decided on the latter, but insisted that Slavonic, not Greek, be the language of the liturgy. Thus he at once opened the door to intensive, prolonged Byzantine influence on Russia but, by retaining Slavonic, assured a clear-cut national identity."

Even in introducing the gentle doctrines of Christianity to the Kiev Rus, Vladimir—called the Holy—demonstrated a certain Viking strength of purpose. According to one report, he drove the entire population into the Dnieper for mass baptism after a guard of his soldiers had dragged down and clubbed the idol Perun, or Thor, and thrown it into the river.

Under Yaroslav the Wise, who recruited several hundred Swedish Vikings to wrest the throne of Kiev from an elder brother in 1019, the Rus court attained its Golden Age. Firmly controlling the trade routes, Yaroslav filled the treasury with the profits of the lively north-south commerce. He chose a Swedish prin-cess, Ingigerd, for his wife, and welcomed Scandinavian royalty—King Olaf the Stout of Norway, his son Magnus, and Olaf's half-brother, Harald Hardraada—to his court. The fame of Kiev spread throughout Europe, and Yaroslav's off-spring became prized royal consorts—so much so that Kievans grumbled at the shortage of brides: "Every European king," went a common saying, "marries a princess of Kiev."

And apparently—to the wonderment of the West—the princesses proved to be literate, a rare attainment among the royalty of that age. One of Yaroslav's daughters, Anna, married Henry I of France and, when widowed, became regent for her son, Philip I. A French official document of 1063 bears the usual assem-blage of crosses and X's penned by French statesmen unable to write their own names. Only one signature appears: in proud Cyrillic characters, it reads *Ana Reina*, Anna the Queen.

I found a few, but very few, reminders of the Vikings in Kiev. I visited the imposing Cathedral of St. Sophia built by Yaroslav between 1037 and 1067. But the church, with its glowing mosaics of sad-eyed saints, represents the north-ward march of Byzantium, not the southward thrust of Sweden.

Later, I strolled down the principal thoroughfare: Kreshchatik, or Christen-ing, Street, so named for that day when all Kiev followed it to the river to be baptized. A show window of the GUM department store displayed three stylized dragon ships, sails set and scudding toward the passerby, crammed with typical products of the Ukraine—ceramics, embroidery, wooden tableware, dolls. Another store offered for sale mass-produced ceramic statuettes of three armed and armored Vikings holding high the banner of Kiev Rus.

The Vikings have long since vanished from their old fief. But, in small ways, Kiev still remembers.

As early as 860, when the Rus first attacked Constantinople, the fighting qualities of the northern warriors had won the admiration of the Byzantine emperors. As a consequence, one provision of a treaty signed in 911 permitted the recruiting of Rus mercenaries for the imperial army. Eventually, these Vikings coalesced into one of the most colorful and valiant corps in all of military history —the Varangian Guard.

Not only from Russia, but from all of Scandinavia and as far as Iceland, did Vikings journey to Miklagård to enlist under the standard of New Rome. The Varangians led the assault in the field and, at home, served as the emperor's personal guard. A tour of duty among the Greeks became a matter of great prestige throughout the North. A boulder found at Ed, near Stockholm, bears the proud message:

> *Ragnvald let the runes be cut.*
> *He was in Greece,*
> *He was leader of the host.*

Harald Hardraada counted it an honor to have commanded the Varangian Guard before mounting the throne of Norway. And a saga tells of the Icelander, Bolli Bollasson, who sailed home after having been a member of the Guard: "He had a gilded helmet on his head and a red shield at his side on which a knight was traced in gold. He carried a lance in his hand, as is the custom in foreign lands. Wherever they took lodgings for the night, the womenfolk paid no heed to anything but to gaze at Bolli and his companions and all their finery."

But a Viking could find something other than glory in Miklagård. Many a runestone in Scandinavia mourns a warrior who *vard daudr i Grikkium*—"died among the Greeks."

Anna Comnena, daughter of Emperor Alexius I Comnenus who reigned at the turn of the 12th century, wrote: "As for the Varangians, who bear on their shoulders the heavy iron sword, they regard loyalty to the emperors and the protection of their persons as a family tradition, a kind of sacred trust and inheritance handed down from generation to generation; this allegiance they preserve inviolate and will never brook the slightest hint of betrayal."

Swords slung across their shoulders, the "ax-bearing barbarians" fought the battles of the empire from Sicily to Syria. After 1066, the Guard underwent a gradual change; with the fall of England to William the Conqueror, more and more Anglo-Saxons and Anglo-Danes avoided the Norman yoke by fleeing to Constantinople and enlisting.

Flames kindled by the nearest relative climb the hull of a dead chieftain's ship. "We burn him in a moment," a Viking once told an Arab witnessing a funeral, "so that he enters Paradise at once."

Indeed, in time the Guard became almost completely anglicized. A 14th-century document, describing ceremonies in the imperial palace, details how the important personages paid their respects to the emperor, followed by the Varangians who greeted him in their own language — "and this was English" — clashing their weapons with a loud noise. Writing in the 12th century, the historian Ordericus Vitalis noted that the English warriors in Byzantium "even to the present day have been dear to Caesar, to the Senate, and to the People."

In 1203, the Franks of the Fourth Crusade interrupted their pious mission to besiege Constantinople. One of them, Villehardouin, described an attack: "The French planted two scaling ladders. . . . The wall here was strongly manned by Englishmen and Danes, and the struggle that ensued was stiff and hard and fierce. By dint of strenuous effort two knights and two sergeants managed to scale the ladders and make themselves masters of the wall. A good 15 of our men got up on top, and were quickly engaged in a hand-to-hand contest of battle-axes against swords." In this action, the axes of the Varangians prevailed. And when the Crusaders sent four envoys to the imperial palace, they found that "the Greeks had posted Englishmen and Danes, equipped with battle-axes, at the gate and right up to the main door of the palace."

After that, we catch only a few glimmers of the Guard in the gathering dusk of Byzantine history. In 1329, a writer refers to "the Varangians with their axes," charged with protecting the keys of any city where the emperor was visiting.

Were there Varangians yet in Constantinople on the fateful day of May 29, 1453, when the Turks crushed the city and, with it, Byzantine civilization? Although no one can be certain, it is unlikely. For, in its twilight, Miklagård had slipped into poverty and neglect. In effect, the boundaries of the empire were the walls of the city. The population had shrunk to 60,000; grass overgrew the cobblestone streets; palaces and churches had fallen into semi-ruin and entwining vines crept from chinks in their walls. The exhausted treasury could support few mercenaries.

Yet, when the end finally came to the Roman state, which had lasted in its various transformations for almost 2,000 years, it came with a certain sunset splendor. In the early spring of 1453, Sultan Mehmet II ringed the city with an enormous Turkish host. Led by the emperor, a tiny force gallantly defended the walls for almost two months, even withstanding artillery barrages. But the end was inevitable. On the night of May 28, amid flickering candles and votive lamps, the emperor attended service in Hagia Sophia; it was the last time that Christians would ever gather in that mighty fortress of God.

"The defenders of the city," wrote an eyewitness, "embraced each other, and through tears kissed one another, asking and giving mutual pardon; no one thought more of wife, child or property, but only of the glorious death which all were ready to meet. . . ."

And meet it they did, before dawn on the walls and at the gates. The last Emperor of the Romans perished sword in hand, leading a forlorn counter-

attack. In some respects he was the noblest of the Byzantine rulers, and his fall the most tragic. He died with the empire as his winding sheet, the shattered city for his sepulcher. Ironically, he bore the same name as the city's founder: Constantine.

A few days later, after the slaughter and the looting, the sultan — henceforth to be known as Mehmet the Conqueror — took possession of the imperial palace. As he contemplated its empty, half-ruined interior, he recited a couplet:

> *The spider spins his web in the Palace of the Caesars,*
> *And the owl sings her watchsong on the towers of Afrasiab.*

His words were the epitaph of imperial Rome. Constantinople that day became, and has remained, the chief city of the Turks. But in 1930 the proud name perished; Turkey rechristened the metropolis Istanbul. Still, a few relics of the distant past survive: the aqueduct, the city walls, the distinctive column and obelisks rising from the grassy park that now marks the site of the hippodrome.

And Hagia Sophia, now a museum.

From the outside, the cathedral — mottled saffron in color — seems a squat jungle of domes and buttresses. Indeed, the only touch of grace stems from the four slender minarets erected by the Turkish conquerors, who converted it into a mosque. But inside, when you step from the gloom of the narthex into the vast nave, the impact is awesome. Shafts of sunlight from the artfully placed windows splash across marble walls, marble floors, marble columns. Insistently, the eye is drawn to the huge dome. Its surface a splendor of golden mosaic, it seems to soar heavenward, carrying the entire structure with it. No wonder Justinian, upon completing Hagia Sophia, cried, "I have surpassed you, O Solomon!"

In the South Gallery, I found the only memento of the Varangians extant in Istanbul: a few runes carved on the marble balustrade. Much defaced by time and other overlapping graffiti, the runes are indecipherable save for the name "Halvdan," presumably the Varangian who carved them long ago.

Leaving the church, I started down the winding, cobbled streets of the Stamboul district toward the harbor, that famed inlet called the Golden Horn. Just as I glanced back toward Hagia Sophia, the rays of the sinking sun caught it broadside. Suddenly the shabby saffron walls flamed and smoldered like molten gold. But as the sun sank further, angles shifted, the fire died; in its wake, the cathedral hulked against the sky like a giant cinder.

Looking at it, I felt a surge of regret for times past, for glory lost. Of mighty Miklagård, only Hagia Sophia endures intact—noble, solitary, sad. The empire is gone, vanished like a dream. The imperial city that wore this church like a diadem of God is no more than a name remembered, a scattering of ruins. No Varangian defends the crumbling walls. The wind off the Bosporus sighs a lonely requiem. The Caesars sleep.

Ingredients for a Viking feast: A hare, a spray of mountain cranberries, dried fish, and a leg of mutton hang on the wall; containers hold spareribs and leeks, curds, wild apples and nuts, mushrooms, cloudberries, peas, herring, and flatbread.

Soapstone weights keep linen warp threads taut on a standing loom in Fitjar, Stord, Norway. Berta Liarbø and her mother, Lina, fashion about five rugs or bedcovers a year. Nearly every Viking wife did her own weaving on a similar loom. Half-knotting (right) keeps warp threads separated. Swedish jewelry of the 10th and 11th centuries—necklace, brooches, bracelets, and a ring—reflects clever craftsmanship.

MUSEUM OF NATIONAL ANTIQUITIES, STOCKHOLM

Art of Viking boatbuilding lives on in the hands of Alfred Søvik of
Lysekloster, Norway. Working without plans, he builds small, graceful
craft for fishermen and sportsmen. Here in his shop, braces secure a
growing hull that when complete will consist of just three wide, thin planks
on each side, held together by rivets. With his keen-bladed, hand-forged
ax (opposite, upper), he shaves a paper-thin curl from a plank. At right,
the afternoon sun spotlights one of his boats moored in Lyse Fjord.

HANS KRISTIAN BUKHOLM

Placid waters of Lake Mälaren rim the island 18 miles west of Stockholm
where the Vikings established Birka, their most important center for trade
with the East. Archeologists began digging here late in the 19th century
and have unearthed hoards of Arabian silver in raw strips, coins, and bracelets.
The double-edged sword, its source unknown, has a pommel of silver inlay.

*S*ymbolic boats of stone fill a Viking Age graveyard in Denmark. At Jelling
in central Jutland, artist Jørn Bie copies the design of the larger
Jelling stone, placed here about 980 by Harald Bluetooth to honor
his parents. The smaller stone bears the word "Danmark," its earliest
appearance in native sources: "Denmark's birth certificate," said Mr. Bie.

B*eneath lowering clouds, kayaks on the Volkhov River glide and dip*
past the walled Russian city of Novgorod. By the tenth century, Vikings
controlled much of northwestern and western Russia; Norse princes ruled in
Novgorod and in Kiev. From there traders journeyed down the Dnieper
to the Black Sea and Constantinople; others followed the Volga to the
Caspian Sea, to trade with the Arab world. About 912 the Northmen captured
Baku, on the Caspian, where women today shop for pomegranates.

Proclaiming peace, Oleg, Prince of Kiev, hangs his shield on the gate of Constantinople

With a convincing show of force he had won a trade treaty favorable to the Northmen.

Crude runes, perhaps the work of one of the Varangian Guard, still scar the marble of Istanbul's Hagia Sophia. The twig-shaped characters, carved on a polished balustrade, are illegible except for the name "Halvdan." Another Viking far from home chiseled ribbons of runes on a marble lion as it stood guard over the port of Athens.

By order of converted King Vladimir, the populace of Kiev wades into the Dnieper for baptism

A peasant watches in wonder as Perun, or Thor—now a discarded wooden idol—bobs past.

RAIDERS: THE TEMPTING

uring the centuries the Vikings of Sweden were coursing the Varangian Way to Kiev and Constantinople — to wealth and glory and, ultimately, to their own ethnic extinction — the Danes and Norwegians were harrying the coasts and river valleys of western Europe. The British Isles, seagirt and misty, with emerald fields and prosperous towns, drew the plunderers like a magnet. Starved for land, Norwegians first settled in the Shetlands and Orkneys. Then, doubling the northern hook of Scotland and pausing to colonize the Hebrides, they sent their dragon ships scudding down the Irish Sea. On the Isle of Man they established a dominion that outlasted the Viking Age, and to our own day the Manx observe certain Norse customs.

But Ireland was the prime Norwegian target. The chronicles paint a lurid picture: "The sea spewed forth floods of foreigners over Erin, so that no haven, no landing-place, no stronghold, no fort, no castle might be found, but it was submerged by waves of vikings and pirates."

As elsewhere in the West, monasteries and churches felt the earliest and cruelest slashes of the heathen sword. The Irish monastic foundation on Iona — which probably produced the magnificently illuminated Book of Kells, a masterpiece of Celtic art — was overrun by Vikings in 795 and again in 801. Returning to the island once more in 806, the raiders slaughtered 68 monks; the survivors fled to the Irish mainland.

So devastating and frequent were the attacks that only bad weather, it sometimes seemed, brought surcease. A ninth-century Irish monk penned a couplet in the margin of a manuscript:

> There's a wicked wind tonight, wild upheaval in the sea;
> No fear now that the Viking hordes will terrify me.

As the century advanced, the Northmen struck in ever greater strength. In 837, some 60 longships entered the mouth of the Boyne and yet another 60 sailed up the Liffey. A later historian detailed the woes of Ireland: "They made spoil-land and sword-land and conquered land of her, throughout her breadth and generally; and they ravaged her chieftainries and her privileged churches and her sanctuaries; and they rent her shrines and her reliquaries and her books."

Ireland, Christian for three centuries before the advent of the Vikings, even saw the great religious shrine of Clonmacnoise defiled when Ota, wife of the Norse leader Turgeis, performed pagan rites before the high altar. An audacious pirate, Turgeis scourged the north, took the monastic settlement of Armagh, and proclaimed himself "King of all Foreigners in Erin." His reign was short. The Irish captured him in 845 and drowned him in Loch Owel.

Turgeis had built what would soon become Dublin on a bank of the Liffey; there in 853 two sons of a minor Norwegian ruler — Olaf and Ivar — established a Norse kingdom destined to endure for more than two centuries. Not far from the center of modern Dublin, archeologists have uncovered the remains of the original settlement. A high fence of corrugated iron, just opposite the Gothic

COASTS

AFTER PICTURE STONE AT LÄRBRO, GOTLAND, SWEDEN

"Tall as date palms, blond and ruddy," an Arab visitor described the

Vikings—one of whose legends the background pictorial carvings illustrate.

His sword red with a bishop's blood, the wily Hasteinn steps from his coffin

in Luna, which he had entered in a mock funeral cortege. He and his

followers then sacked the city, thinking they had captured fabled Rome.

splendor of Christ Church Cathedral, protects this portal into the past. Breandán Ó Ríordáin, Assistant Keeper of Irish Antiquities and supervisor of the excavation, showed me through his dig.

"We had to penetrate 14 feet of debris to reach the original level," he told me, "and some of it is unmistakably Viking."

I noticed that the first streets had been constructed of heavy timbers in the fashion of every Viking town uncovered. The jammed-together houses once sheltered merchants and craftsmen. "A combmaker lived here," said Mr. Ó Ríordáin, pointing to an irregular floor plan outlined by remains of a wicker-work and mud-daub wall. "We found the antlers he used as raw material, blanks he had carved, and even a few finished products. Other workers in bone produced gaming pieces and whistles. Over there lived a shoemaker, to judge from the leather scraps. We've found brooches, pins, weights, and even a mold for casting silver hammers—the symbol of Thor. Many of the finds are identical to artifacts from sites in Scandinavia. Not until the 11th-century strata do we detect a merging of Norse and Irish cultures."

Later I spoke to Dr. A. T. Lucas, Director of the National Museum of Ireland, who thinks that history has overblackened the Vikings' name. "You must remember," he said, "that in the Middle Ages churches served as sanctuaries for goods as well as persons. Anyone could bring his valuables to the priests for safekeeping. The churches served, if you will, as the banks of medieval Europe. And I believe that Vikings were by no means the only ones to loot them.

"The various Irish annals list 309 occasions on which ecclesiastical sites were plundered between 600 and 1163 A.D. Where the nationality of the plundering party is known, the Irish were responsible on 139 occasions and the Norse on 140, while on 19 occasions the plundering was carried out by the Irish and Norse in combination. Clearly, then, the Irish were as deeply implicated as the Norsemen."

Although the Vikings controlled the harbors of Ireland until the 11th century, they had little success in conquering the country as a whole. The Irish political system—based upon numerous *túaths*, tiny areas ruled by kings of local clans—foredoomed any campaign of conquest. Winning victories over the minor kings was easy enough, but consolidating their domains was another matter. Lacking the manpower to occupy every túath in Ireland, the Vikings stuck to their coastal strongholds.

They took some consolation, however, in raiding across the Irish Sea, and in 919 succeeded in conquering the Danish Kingdom of York. The Dublin-York-Scandinavian trade axis thrived; but Norse rule in York was continually threatened by the increasing power of the English kings.

The Viking invasion of Erin caused the Irish gradually to forsake their traditional tribal pattern and—in order to oppose the Vikings—to develop something akin to unity. Thus in 1014 Brian Boru, the first effective High King of Ireland, was able to defeat the Vikings in a climactic battle at Clontarf. Although the Norse remained and even ruled locally for another generation or two, Clontarf effectively destroyed their domination of Ireland.

Not everyone Irish had been loyal to Brian, as it turned out. Although the "fairest and best-gifted" Gormflaith had taken him as her third husband, she was quite ready to desert him and give her hand to Sigurd, a Viking chieftain. But Sigurd fell in battle; and after Clontarf, the indiscreet Gormflaith disappears from the annals.

Along with such intrigues, there were firm and open friendships across the lines drawn by invaders and defenders. As one might expect of two peoples so enthralled by poetry, these often involved Irish bards and Norse skalds. A bard from Munster says in his elegy for his murdered master that it is hard to condemn the Viking instigator entirely, because of his own friendship for the Norseman's son. And Brian Boru's chief poet spent a year at the court of Sigtrygg Silkbeard in Dublin.

One searches in vain for any permanent imprint of the Viking Age on Irish life. Perversely enough, Irish tradition even identifies the occupiers as Danes, rather than the Norwegians that most of them actually were. A few family names hark back—Searson to Sigurdsson and Sugrue to Siegfried—and two persistent folk beliefs: that the Danes brewed the finest beer ever tasted in Erin, and that foxes—those predatory and destructive animals—are Danish dogs spitefully left behind when Brian Boru drove their masters out of Ireland.

On the 221-square-mile Isle of Man, situated in the Irish Sea almost midway between the coasts of England and Erin, the Norwegians sank deeper roots. A Viking burial dating from the second half of the ninth century indicates that Norse invaders not only had seized the land from the Celtic inhabitants but, soon reverting to their original occupations, had also begun to farm it. In 1946 archeologists uncovered fragments of a man's skeleton with all the gear of a Viking warrior; a young woman and the usual domestic animals had been slain to accompany him. Over the whole, mourners had fashioned a proper mound composed of layers of turf. But soil analysis revealed that the turf came from several other parts of the island. The archeologists concluded that the dead man had been a farmer, and that he had been buried beneath sod gathered from his own fields.

The Norse institution of the *Althing* — an annual meeting of freeholders to promulgate laws and to render judgments — still survives on Man, though the isle has long been subject to the British Crown. Not far from the capital, Douglas, a low mound rises from a grassy plot facing ancient St. John's Church. Here each year on Midsummer Day, July 5, Manxmen gather for the Tynwald. The word comes from the Old Norse *Thingvöllr,* or Assembly Field, and the proceeding — with occasional lapses — has been a vital feature of Manx life for more than a thousand years. An excerpt from the diary of a Manxman who emigrated to America early in the last century sums up the local reverence for both site and ceremony: "This morning, before daylight, I stole away to St. John's, for to see one last time the ancient ceremonies on Tynwald Hill, and secretly to take from its lowest round, one little handful of that earth which has seen, maybe, and heard more history than any other spot on the Island."

Norwegians had been marauding for almost two generations when, in the year 834, Danish Vikings appeared in force. Generally leaving the Irish Sea to their cousins from the fjords, the Danes concentrated their attention on both shores of the English Channel. Over and over again they raided Frisia — roughly the present-day Netherlands — and soon mounted a major attack on Dorestad. This Frisian city preceded Hedeby as a major trading center and even boasted its own mint. The Vikings left it a smoldering wasteland.

In France the Danes sailed up the Loire River and sacked Nantes; moving up the Seine, they attacked Paris repeatedly. Three times they sacked it. The Frankish kings, busy defending their troubled land frontiers, were unable to keep an effective military force patrolling the coasts and rivers, and the Vikings roamed virtually at will.

Only miracles could save the helpless citizenry; sometimes, according to legend, they came to pass. Thus, in Chartres, I visited the treasury of the famed cathedral to see the Veil of the Virgin. This length of cloth, reputedly worn by Mary, the mother of Jesus, is said to have reached France in the ninth century as a gift from the Empress of Byzantium. Then, as now, it ranked as one of the most precious relics of Christendom. A tradition in Chartres holds that when the fierce Northmen sailed up the Eure River the bishop repelled them by bravely waving the veil from the city walls.

And perhaps it did happen — once. But Chartres fell to the Danes, as did virtually every city of consequence in the realm. People began to wonder if perhaps these calamities were God's punishment for their sins. King Charles the Bald issued a royal declaration:

"Our country is a desert; the inhabitants having been killed or put to flight, because we have killed ourselves with the sword of sin. Churches and villages have been burned because we have lit the flame of avarice, of rapacity, of the most impure passions.... It is God who chastises us.... Do penance therefore through confession and through alms."

France suffered severely, but tragedy struck both ways. The Vikings, throughout the age, endured fearful casualties. A Swedish runestone preserves the history of one family:

The good farmer Gulle had five sons:
At Fyris fell Åsmund, the unfrightened warrior,
Assur died out east in Greece,
Halvdan was in duel slain,
Kare died at [Dundee?]. Dead is Boe too.

Originally, the Northmen had gone viking only in the summer, returning each winter to their farms. But the middle of the ninth century saw them taking up semipermanent residence in certain French rivers, wintering near the mouths and roaming inland in the fine weather. Chroniclers even began to write of the "Loire Vikings" and the "Seine Vikings."

Meanwhile, the Danish *drekar*, or dragon ships, pressed on down the coasts of Europe, finally reaching the Iberian Peninsula. The Moors, followers of Mohammed who had poured across the Strait of Gibraltar in 711, held all but a few northern sectors of Spain and Portugal. After a century of consolidating their domain, the Emirs of Córdoba, rulers of the peninsula, had fashioned the most advanced state on the continent. Their cities—Granada, Seville, Jaen— gleamed white among fertile fields and orchards. Toledo was a center of learning, Lisbon a center of commerce. But in southern Spain, Moorish civilization reached its apogee. Here the warm Mediterranean washed sandy beaches; inland rose the lofty peaks of the Sierra Morena and the Sierra Nevada. This perfect province bore the name al-Andaluz, and throughout the far-flung realms of Islam the faithful believed that Paradise was located in the sky directly above it.

The Moors advanced the sciences of medicine and mathematics; alone in western Europe, they preserved and studied the Greek classics, including Plato and Aristotle. Poets sang beside cool fountains, and their rhymes helped inspire the verses of the troubadours who were soon to intoxicate Provence and the courts of Europe. So redoubtable were the Moorish armies, so vigilant the fleet, that citizens didn't trouble to surround their cities with fortifications.

The agreeable, prosperous land of Andaluz had thoroughly beguiled the desert raiders who had conquered it. Spain soon ameliorated even the harshest doctrines of the Prophet: wine, forbidden by the Koran, was much admired and indeed much consumed by the Moors; Granada craftsmen used human figures in fabrics and ivory carvings, despite the prohibition on portraits as graven images. In the golden ninth century, the princes and poets of Andaluz passed

their days in learning and in leisure. Sunset brought its special, sultry pleasures:

> *How many nights have I lingered in your shadows*
> *With girls . . . both blonde and dusky,*
> *Who pierced my soul*
> *Like blazing swords, like somber lances.*

Into this sophisticated society the Danes burst like a thunderclap. The first recorded incursion came in the year 844. Moorish chroniclers, rigidly monotheistic, affixed a contemptuous name to the pagan Northmen: *al-Magus*, fire worshipers. After long contemplation, Sa'id, a jurist of Toledo, gave this judgment of the barbarians: "Because the sun does not shed its rays directly over their heads, their climate is cold and the atmosphere clouded. Consequently their temperaments have become cold and their humours rude, while their bodies have grown large, their complexions light and their hair long. They lack withal sharpness of wit and penetration of intellect, while stupidity and folly prevail among them."

Of that first Viking appearance off the Iberian coast, a Moor recorded that "al-Magus arrived with about eighty vessels which covered the sea like so many red and black birds, and filled all hearts with anguish and anxiety. . . ."

After a series of engagements the Danes sailed up the Guadalquivir and occupied Seville, where they slaughtered indiscriminately, even killing a coterie of aged men who had sought refuge in a mosque. This sacrilege outraged the Moors, and they perpetuated its memory in a new name for the sanctuary, *Masdjid al-Shuhada'*, or Mosque of the Martyrs.

Under watchful Arab eyes, longships of a marauding fleet led by

Hasteinn and Bjørn cruise the unfamiliar Mediterranean. In Morocco they

spent a week ashore rounding up prisoners for ransom or sale as slaves.

In the Moorish capital of Córdoba, the Emir Abd al-Rahman II lost no time in raising reinforcements. A corps of light cavalry and a column of infantry advanced upon Seville, harassing the Northmen and inflicting severe losses. Then, on November 11, the Danes poured forth from their ships in the river to face the Moors in a decisive battle. The foes clashed on a plain south of the city called Tablada, now the site of an airport. The vengeful Moors won a swift and pitiless victory, slaying more than a thousand Northmen and capturing 400.

In panic, the surviving Danes bolted for their ships and strained at the oars to reach the safety of the mouth of the Guadalquivir. On the bank, the Moors methodically killed the prisoners under the eyes of their fleeing comrades; they then burned 30 ships that failed to escape.

Far from successful, this massive Viking raid nevertheless ended on a disarming note. Several parties of Danes had been foraging in the hinterland of Seville when the final battle was joined, and their shipmates precipitously abandoned them. Soon overtaken by the victorious Moslems, these remnants — perhaps to save their souls, but surely to save their lives — promptly embraced Islam. Settling outside the towns of Carmona and Morón, they applied themselves to an age-old Danish specialty: dairy farming. For generations to come, they furnished the markets of Seville and Córdoba with what a French historian hailed as "cheeses of repute."

But Spain had not seen the last of the Vikings. About 859 a chieftain named Hasteinn and his co-leader Bjørn led 62 ships from France on an epic viking voyage — one immortalized by chroniclers both Christian and Moslem.

Following the shoreline to the Bay of Biscay, they proceeded to loot the Iberian coast in leisurely fashion, pausing long enough in the shadow of the Rock of Gibraltar to sack the neighboring Moorish city of Algeciras and burn down the Grand Mosque. Then, perhaps for the first time, the dragon ships of the North nosed into the mild blue waters of the Mediterranean.

Unopposed, the raiders ranged the North African littoral. A Moslem chronicler recorded their visit to Nekor, not far from Mellilla. "Al-Magus — may God curse them! — invaded the city of Nekor and pillaged it. They took into captivity all the inhabitants with the exception of those who saved their lives by flight." Among their prisoners in North Africa, the Vikings derived singular delight from the first Negroes — they called them "blue men" — that they had ever seen.

Marauding as they went, Hasteinn and his followers coasted eastern Spain, ravaged the Balearics and southern France, and wintered pleasantly in the delta of the Rhône River. Systematically they despoiled all the significant cities of the region, including Arles and Nîmes. Sailing on to Italy, they put Pisa to sword and brand. Then, relates the possibly apocryphal account of the French monk William of Jumièges — who refers to Hasteinn as Hastings — adverse winds blew the Danish fleet to the city of Luna, on the coast between Pisa and Genoa. Dazzled by its towering walls and marble buildings, Hasteinn believed he had found Rome itself:

"The citizens, astonished by the arrival of such a fleet, barricaded the gates of their city.... [Hastings] set himself to seek *(Continued on page 92)*

*M*iniature fjord serves pristine Gjógv on Eysturoy in the
Faeroes, North Atlantic island group the Vikings colonized in the ninth
century. At right, fishermen of nearby Eidi get a predawn start.
Dangling on a rope held by companions, a Skúvoy islander uses a
bag at the end of his pole to gather eggs of the cliff-dwelling
guillemots. Limits on collecting assure survival of the bird colony.

Thrashing in confusion, pilot whales allow Faeroese boatmen to herd them into the Tindhólmur shallows of Vágar Island. Following age-old custom, the men will then slaughter and divide the catch.

Snug cottage of a Shetland Islands farmer, or crofter, hugs the earth at Sandness. A rope network secures the thatch above low walls; the floor lies below ground level, and those who enter must stoop. Small windows in the walls and roof let in the daylight. Until a century ago, crofters used oil lamps like the early-medieval soapstone vessel at right.

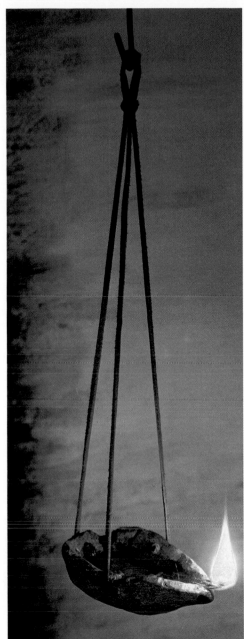

SHETLAND COUNTY MUSEUM

Woman keeps a milch goat under firm control at Jarlshof in the Shetlands, one of the earliest

farm complexes established by westward-migrating Norsemen. Sumburgh Head shelters the bay.

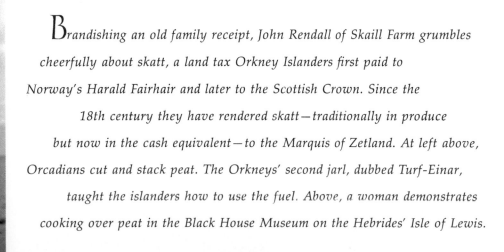

*Brandishing an old family receipt, John Rendall of Skaill Farm grumbles
cheerfully about skatt, a land tax Orkney Islanders first paid to
Norway's Harald Fairhair and later to the Scottish Crown. Since the
18th century they have rendered skatt—traditionally in produce
but now in the cash equivalent—to the Marquis of Zetland. At left above,
Orcadians cut and stack peat. The Orkneys' second jarl, dubbed Turf-Einar,
taught the islanders how to use the fuel. Above, a woman demonstrates
cooking over peat in the Black House Museum on the Hebrides' Isle of Lewis.*

with the utmost diligence how he might make himself master of the city by arti-
fice. Finally, sending to the bishop and to the count . . . he had the ministers of
his perfidy declare that he had landed in these parts with no design, and that
his sole desire was to return to his own country; that he wished and asked only
for peace, and that he himself, stricken with a mortal illness, humbly implored
them to baptize him a Christian. . . .

"Finally, the villainous Hastings was transported to the church; the man full
of guile was sprinkled with the sacred waters of baptism. . . . after having been
anointed with holy chrism, he was carried to his ship in the arms of his men. . . .

"Hastings had himself placed in a coffin and gave orders to his companions
to don armor beneath their tunics. Immediately, great lamentations were heard
throughout the army along with the report that Hastings, the new convert, had
just died. . . . He was carried out of his ship and conducted to the church. The
bishop clothed himself in his sacred vestments and prepared to sacrifice the
Most Holy Host in honor of the deceased. Prayers were chanted for his soul, in
order that his body, burdened with wickedness, dedicated to perdition and already enclosed in the coffin, might become worthy of Christian burial.

"But behold, Hastings leaps out of his coffin and slays with his sword both
bishop and count! Thereafter, he and his followers, taking the people unawares,
glut their frenzy like devouring wolves. The house of God becomes the theater
of crimes committed by His deadly enemy; the young are massacred, the throats
of the old are cut, the city devastated. . . ."

Only then did Hasteinn learn, "amid the glad congratulation," that the
prize he had taken was not the Eternal City after all.

A little more than a mile inland from the seaside resorts of Italy's Apuana
Riviera, protected by the headland of La Spezia to the west and a rugged mountain range to the east, I found the remains of Luna. It is of brilliant white marble
still, but the fragments are scattered across the flat green fields. A small museum
houses statues and inscriptions excavated on the site. The shell of an impressive
amphitheater still stands, as does the principal gate and the granary and the
ruined forum. Vikings did indeed raid this coast in the ninth century, and perhaps more than once. So did Saracens and Lombards. All contributed to the
downfall of a city that had already marked 1,500 years of history when Hasteinn
appeared at its gates.

Nature struck the final blow. Gradually the harbor silted, destroying Luna's
trade in marble from the nearby Carrara quarries. Mosquitoes infested the
marshy remains, bringing malaria. By 1200 the city was known as *La Maledetta*,
The Accursed, and the population had fled. Petrarch wrote Luna's epitaph:
"Once famous and powerful and now only naked and without a name."

From Luna, Hasteinn may have led his vessels farther to the east, even perhaps as far as Alexandria. But, unfortunately for the Danes, home lay through
the Strait of Gibraltar—where awaiting the Vikings' inevitable return cruised
a Moorish fleet with a score to settle.

With no real alternative, Hasteinn dared the passage. The Moors exacted a
fearful toll of men and ships, and refurbished the doors of the Algeciras mosque

with strong northern timber from the vessels they captured. The mauled Danes beat northward at top speed; they did, however, pause in Navarre to capture Pamplona and extort a huge ransom for the return of its prince. Finally, in 862, the battered fleet once more dropped anchor in its French home port. Two-thirds of the original 62 ships had been lost, but Hasteinn, Bjørn, and their surviving Vikings had gained wealth and glory in heaping measure.

Though the Danes struck hard at the European continent, England felt the fullest fury of their assaults. As the ninth century advanced, the early raiders gave way to well-organized Danish fleets and armies bent on conquest and colonization. In 850, relates the Anglo-Saxon Chronicle, "the heathen for the first time remained over the winter." Successively London, Rochester, Canterbury, and Winchester felt the violence of the invaders.

Only King Alfred the Great, who reigned in Wessex, proved capable of resisting and even defeating them. He went so far as to best the Vikings at their own game. According to the Chronicle, "King Alfred had 'long ships' built to oppose the Danish warships. They were almost twice as long as the others. Some had 60 oars, some more. They were both swifter and steadier and also higher than the others. They were built neither on the Frisian nor the Danish pattern, but as it seemed to himself that they could be most useful." In 896, when Alfred's new fleet first appeared, it promptly captured two Viking ships and disabled two. By the end of summer, 20 Danish vessels, "men and all, perished along the south coast."

While Alfred ensured that there would continue to be an England, he could not drive the Danes from the northeastern third of the country. There they "shared out the lands . . . and were engaged in ploughing and making a living for themselves." The Vikings set up two kingdoms — one centered upon York, the other in East Anglia, and they ruled as well in the intervening area known as the five boroughs: Stamford, Leicester, Derby, Nottingham, and Lincoln. Because Danish law and custom prevailed here, this region — bordered on the north at first by the River Tees, later by the River Tweed, and on the southwest by a line running roughly from the Thames Estuary east of London to the vicinity of modern Birmingham — became known as the Danelaw.

Most of the Danes, who hungered for land even more than for loot, settled down happily to farm their new fields. Even though Alfred's successors began to win back control over the Danelaw, they carefully refrained from altering its special character. In fact, its peculiar criminal law procedures survived well into the Middle Ages, as did the system of coin denominations which spread beyond the Danelaw and became the basis for the medieval currency of England.

Certain linguistic legacies of the Danelaw linger still. The Old Norse suffixes -*by* (town) and -*thorp* (outlying settlement) identify former Viking habitations. So "Danby" — what could sound more English? — proves to be Old Norse for "Danetown," and "Hackenthorpe" was once "Hakon's Farm." That greatest of horse races, the Derby, has a Norse root; so do numerous words of the Yorkshire dialect, such as *beck* (stream), *force* (waterfall), and *fell* (hill).

*"*P*eace in exchange for gold!" the Viking ultimatum rings across the*
water. "Come to the slaughter!" reply the Saxons at Maldon—inviting
their own doom; each man then "hewed down until at last he fell himself."

In the old Danelaw, I know towns called Skirpenbeck, Willitoft, and Lumby. In Normandy are other towns called Bolbec, Lintot, and Hambye. Different nations, different cultures, different languages; yet, where they share Viking ancestry, the place names are virtually interchangeable.

Alfred's successors on the throne—his son Edward, who reigned until 924, and then Edward's son Athelstan—proved to be formidable warriors. Edward routed a raiding Danish army in 910, killed Halfdan, the last Danish king of York, and checked Viking power in the north. In 937, the Dublin Vikings made common cause with the Celts of Scotland and invaded England. Athelstan and his brother Edmund met them at Brunanburh and inflicted so devastating a defeat that the Anglo-Saxon Chronicle celebrated it by bursting into verse:

> *With their hammered blades, the sons of Edward*
> *Clove the shield-wall and hacked the linden bucklers . . .*
> *And the host from the ships fell doomed. The field*
> *Grew dark with the blood of men . . . the English king and the prince,*
> *Brothers triumphant in war, together*
> *Returned to their home, the land of Wessex.*

Toward the end of the tenth century, however, the fighting qualities of the line of English kings sired by Alfred died out. In 978 the crown passed to Ethelred Unraed ("Uncounseled," usually mistranslated as "the Unready"). The disastrous 38-year reign of this inept and irresolute monarch spelled the doom of Anglo-Saxon England.

Viking raiders, who had prudently avoided England for a generation, struck again in ever-increasing numbers. Soon entire armies poured ashore. Olaf Tryggvason led the first one in 991. Ethelred then erred fatally; he levied a special tax on his subjects—the *danegeld*, "ransom to the Danes"—and pacified Olaf with the proceeds: 22,000 Saxon pounds of silver (about three-fourths of that weight, or 16,500 pounds, on today's scale).

In response—remembering how profitable the similar extracting of tribute had been in France—Vikings poured from every quarter of the North into England. Olaf returned in 994 with a temporary ally, King Svein Forkbeard of Denmark, to share a danegeld of 16,000 pounds of silver. In 1002 the Danes collected 24,000 pounds; in 1007, 36,000 pounds. According to his saga, Olaf Haraldsson—Norway's future King Olaf the Stout—led a fleet up the Thames, tore down London Bridge with grappling irons, and sailed through the wreckage to plunder all the fair valley beyond.

The Chronicle dutifully details Ethelred's incompetence and its disastrous consequences:

"And when the enemy was in the east, then our levies were mustered in the west; and when they were in the south, then our levies were in the north. . . . Whatever course of action was decided upon it was not followed even for a single month. . . . All these misfortunes befell us by reason of bad policy. . . ."

But not all the Saxons chose Ethelred's road of vacillation and surrender to blackmail. At Maldon in 991, the men of Essex bravely fought a Viking

host. Although the victory went to the Danes, the valor of the Saxon stand gave rise to one of the stateliest of Old English poems, *The Battle of Maldon*. Cries the beleaguered Saxon leader:

> *"Mind must be the firmer, heart the more fierce,*
> *Courage the greater, as our strength diminishes. . . ."*

Ethelred paid his last danegeld in 1012—a staggering 48,000 pounds of silver. But the next year saw Svein Forkbeard once more on the attack. The English could endure no more; Ethelred fled and his people submitted. Svein died soon after, but his son Knut succeeded him, put down a series of disorders—including a brief and predictably ill-starred reappearance of Ethelred—and was acknowledged King of England in 1016.

Knut thereupon extracted a final prodigious danegeld of 83,000 pounds of silver, paid off his troops, and consolidated his rule. Skaldic verses immortalized this Viking monarch who was terrible in battle, pitiless to his enemies, yet withal a just ruler.

> *Gracious giver of mighty gifts, you made corselets red in Norwich. . . .*
> *They could not defend their strongholds when you attacked.*
> *The bow screamed loud.*
> *You won no less renown, driver of the leaping steed of the roller,*
> *On Thames' bank. The wolf's jaw knew this well. . . .*
> *You are swift to deal with the race of men.*

Eventually Knut welded England and most of Scandinavia into a short-lived North Sea Empire, and could characterize himself—as he did in 1027—*Rex totius Angliae et Dennemarchiae et Norregiae et partis Suavorum*, King of all England and Denmark and Norway and part of Sweden.

Some historians theorize that England did not fall to a series of haphazard Viking campaigns, but rather suffered defeat in a 20-year war carefully organized and prosecuted by Svein Forkbeard. The existence in Denmark of four strategically scattered military camps, all dating from about the year 1000, lends weight to the theory. All were constructed to the same rigid geometric pattern, all commanded vital waterways, and all could have served as staging areas for England-bound Vikings.

Archeologists have made extensive excavations at Trelleborg in western Zealand. Lying as it does amid the green serenity of cultivated fields, the Trelleborg camp strikes a visitor like a sudden clang of arms. A massive earthen bulwark rises out of the plain in a huge circle. I climbed to the top of the rampart, more than 55 feet thick and 23 feet high, and surveyed the remains of the Viking camp. My eye traced the outlines of 16 long, boat-shaped barracks arranged in squares of four on the surface of the craterlike interior. Each had probably housed a ship's crew, about 60 to 75 men. To the east and south, outside the great defensive barrier, I could see the remnants of 15 similar buildings defended by an outer bulwark and a moat.

Near the complex, specialists of the National Museum of Denmark have attempted to reproduce one of the boat-shaped barracks. Leaving the rampart—patrolled now only by drifting sheep—I walked to the reproduction and stooped through the low door. Wan, wintry light filtered through the chimney hole in the center of the roof. It lit a rock-lined open hearth below. A wide earthen bench lined the side walls.

Once, a millennium ago, men about to go west-viking to England had lounged on such benches. They had eaten there, quaffed ale, honed their spears, oiled their leather, mended their shields. Skalds had chanted beside the fire, and when the ale and the poetry failed, the warriors had wrapped themselves in their cloaks, stretched out, and slept as the embers died.

I had a peculiar sensation of *déjà vu*. Although I had never been in such a building, it seemed overpoweringly familiar. Then, in a rush of remembrance, I knew why. This long house of another age differed in no essential detail from the quonset huts of my own military service. Cots had lined the corrugated walls like benches; our hearth had been a cast-iron stove in the center of the hut. In the evening, troops preparing for a foreign expedition had lounged on their cots, cleaning rifles, sharpening bayonets, mending equipment. And our own skald, an Oklahoman named Harvey, had sung softly of *The Hills of Home*.

*Small script above and below the rich illumination of the Gospel of
St. Matthew in the eighth-century Codex Aureus reminds posterity that an English
earl ransomed it from Viking raiders "with pure gold . . . for the love of God."*

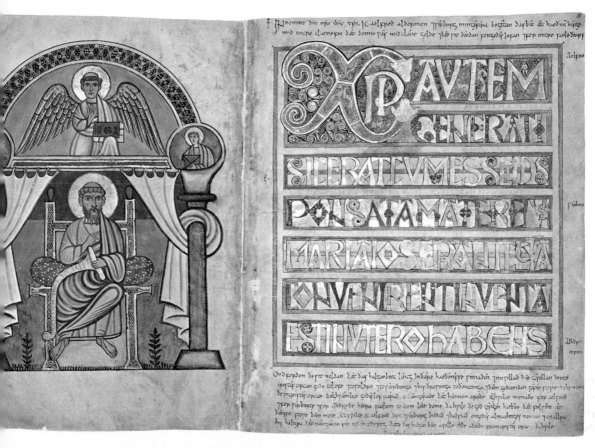

*Viking coins minted in
England and Ireland, and contemporary
accounts such as the Anglo-Saxon
Chronicle passage beneath these
silver pennies, give clues to
the chronology of Scandinavian
settlement of the British Isles.*

Typical Norse timber pathway spans a large dig near High Street, Dublin. Its artifacts include numerous combs; the Vikings took great pride in their long, blond hair. From antler, artisans cut backs and sawed tooth blanks, fitted them together, and sometimes fashioned a protective case.

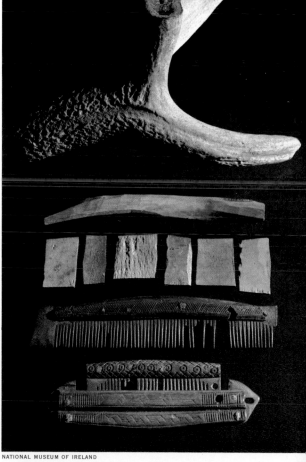

NATIONAL MUSEUM OF IRELAND

Pre-Viking festival customs and contests survive in England's old Danelaw region. A young visitor watches as the men of Barwick-in-Elmet raise the Maypole and deck it with garlands. In Cumberland-Westmorland-style wrestling at Bellingham, the first man to the ground loses.

Jury box in Bury St. Edmunds awaits its occupants. Under England's Norse invaders, 12-man juries gave and heard evidence, and reached verdicts by vote. But the Vikings dealt summarily with East Anglia's King Edmund in 870 when—wrote a biographer—"he refused to forswear his faith"; they tied him to a tree and shot him with arrows. Every November 20 the town's Cathedral Church of St. James commemorates his martyrdom.

Warning from King Alfred: Six Danelaw Vikings captured after a raid

hang as common robbers—a grim example to their fellow invaders.

"Alfred ordered me to be made," reads an inscription on the cloisonné Alfred Jewel; but no one knows whose portrait it bears.

ASHMOLEAN MUSEUM, OXFORD

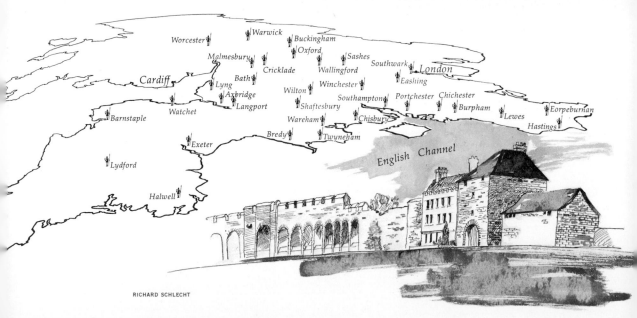

Worcester
Warwick
Buckingham
Malmesbury
Oxford
Cricklade
Sashes
Southwark
London
Cardiff
Wallingford
Bath
Winchester
Eashing
Lyng
Wilton
Axbridge
Southampton
Portchester
Chichester
Watchet
Langport
Shaftesbury
Barnstaple
Wareham
Chisbury
Burpham
Lewes
Eorpeburnan
Hastings
Exeter
Bredy
Twyneham
English Channel
Lydford

Halwell

RICHARD SCHLECHT

Norman West Gate at Southampton, left, stands on the site of a Roman fort Alfred strengthened to protect his palace upriver at Winchester.

In 892 he began to build a series of 33 defenses, no more than 40 miles apart, throughout free England, and organized a peasant militia to man them on regular shifts against the invading Danes. Above, a church the Saxons built at Breamore about the same period still stands.

French workmen harvest salt on the Île de Noirmoutier in the Bay of Biscay. Vikings took over the island as a winter base in 842—"as if they meant to stay forever," wrote one rueful annalist. At left, bulls pick their way across the Rhône delta's Camargue, Hasteinn's winter haven in 859.

Despite fire and massed assaults, the Île de la Cité remains impregnable through a
year-long siege. The Danes attacked Paris in 885 after the French rejected
their offer to spare the city in exchange for unhindered passage up the Seine.
The Vikings destroyed the Left Bank church of St.-Julien-le-Pauvre; the rebuilt church,
in foreground below, dates from the 12th century, as does Notre-Dame, beyond.

he same pressures that drove the Scandinavians to raid and seize territory in Europe and the British Isles — an increasing population and a shortage of arable land — also sent them on their quest for virgin ground. The most mysterious sea-road led west, and for 200 years Norse mariners followed it to probe the North Atlantic. In their small wooden vessels they ventured into new waters that bounded unknown countries. Yet the farthest paths they blazed would, with the end of their age, slip into navigational limbo; their greatest discovery, Vinland, would fade from human ken; their colonies in Greenland would struggle for survival through 500 years and then these, too, would slip into oblivion.

Greed for plunder and greed for fame raged like twin fevers in Norse veins, but hotter still burned the lust for land — for fat pastures and rich soil beside emerald fjords. So, in growing numbers, Northmen loaded their vessels and sought the future beyond the western horizon.

Again in the Atlantic, the key factor in the Vikings' success was the quality of their ships. When raiding, they had exploited the special characteristics of the longship: speed afloat that permitted the lightning blow, the rapid escape; a shallow draft that made them independent of harbors, enabling them to drive ashore on any beach. It is sobering to reflect that no modern navy has been able to devise a landing craft as fast, effective, and seaworthy as a Viking ship of war.

But it was the dragon ship's slower, stockier cousin, the *knarr*, that won the honor of conquering the North Atlantic. Norse merchant vessels had sailed the Baltic Sea and the Russian rivers and made trading landfalls at Birka and Hedeby and Cork, and were — in an economic and social sense — far more vital to Scandinavian prosperity than the glamorous warships. Knarrs, the larger versions of the trading vessels, became the instruments that planted Norse colonies across the northern tier of the world — from the Faeroes to Iceland to Greenland to the forested shores of North America.

From literary sources, scholars had long known that knarrs were broad-beamed, deep-draught cargo ships and had even conjectured — with, it eventually turned out, commendable accuracy — as to their appearance. Then, in one of the surprises that make archeology so delightful a study, an operation that began in 1957 raised actual examples of these homely vessels from a murky undersea grave. It happened near the historic Danish city of Roskilde, once the royal seat of Harald Bluetooth and Svein Forkbeard, which lies at the head of a fjord of the same name. As the Viking Age neared an end, between 1000 and 1050, Roskilde achieved eminence as a trading town. Sometime during that period, invaders posed a threat; and at a narrow channel of the fjord some 12 miles above Roskilde, approximately halfway between the town and the sea, the Danish defenders heaped five ships with stones and scuttled them. Whether or not this artificial barrier repelled the attackers remains unknown; but through the intervening centuries it greatly irritated the fishermen of the Roskilde Fjord, who had to negotiate it carefully. Finally, archeologists arrived on the scene

ROAD WEST

Sea-weathered Icelander's features suggest a Norse-Celtic heritage.
Norse settlers coming from Ireland brought Celts as wives or servants.

after amateur frogmen had brought up a fragment of wood and submitted it to the Danish National Museum.

Between 1957 and 1959, Olaf Olsen and Ole Crumlin-Pedersen of the museum staff made preliminary underwater surveys of the wreckage. Then in 1962 they achieved a spectacular salvage of the crushed, wave-worn remains of all five vessels.

"The excavation introduced several innovations," Mr. Crumlin-Pedersen told me as we toured the magnificent new museum erected in Roskilde to house the ships. "We built a cofferdam around the wreckage and pumped out the water, eliminating the difficulties of underwater work. We also used photogrammetry [measurement by use of vertical photographs] to plot the site, rather than the traditional grid system. Not only is the photogrammetry superior, but a single person can do it all in a few days. The older method required surveying instruments and took months.

"Because we anticipated shrinkage in the wooden fragments, we had an artist sketch every piece on polythene folio, a special plastic that resists aging, stretching, shrinking, and tearing. One man spent five years on this alone."

At the museum, the unhurried work of restoration proceeds beneath the eyes of visitors, now numbering some 150,000 annually. Three specialists work full time fitting together the five mammoth jigsaw puzzles from the past. When no problems arise, they can reconstruct one strake, fore to aft, of one ship in a

Eric the Red falls with his horse in Greenland. He took the

accident as a bad omen, and withdrew from his son Leif's

expedition to the west: "This is as far as we go together." Leif

persevered—and landed on the coast of North America about A.D. *1000.*

week or two. The museum displays the slowly reforming ships in a huge hall; the all-glass northern wall frames them dramatically against the waters of the fjord outside.

"The exciting aspect of this find," Mr. Crumlin-Pedersen explained as we viewed the skeletal vessels from a balcony, "is that we've identified several types: two different warships, and three assorted workaday craft. Now this one," he gestured toward the bare outline of a low, lithe vessel almost 95 feet long, "was a true Viking warship designed to carry 40 to 60 men. It's the larger of the two we found. From the lines, we can tell that it sailed well and swiftly and was light enough to be rowed very fast. The worn state of the keel indicates that it was often dragged ashore. I'd say it's a perfect example of the ships used on foreign raids.

"On the other hand, this," he indicated the partial reconstruction of a capacious craft a little more than 40 feet in length, "was designed to carry bulky and heavy loads. It's built of oak, and probably traded in the Baltic and on Russian rivers. We've recovered about 75 percent of it."

Finally we stopped before a broad, sturdy vessel some 54 feet long, the museum's *pièce de résistance*. "Here is our knarr, a true deep-sea trader that plied the North Atlantic to Iceland and Greenland. Half decks fore and aft provided space for the crew, while cargo, including livestock, was stowed in an open hold amidships. Planks from a similar vessel have been uncovered in a Norse settlement in Greenland."

Even before the electrifying finds in the Roskilde Fjord, a passion for duplicating the products of Viking craftsmanship had been stirring in Denmark. The man who conceived the movement, a dedicated teacher-scoutmaster in the tiny village of Enderupskov in Jutland, is T. Hartvig Nielsen. Tall, blond, and bearded, this engaging nonconformist taught—at his own choice—for almost 20 years in one of the few remaining two-room schools in Denmark. Last year, to the sorrow of both the teacher and his pupils, a larger and more impersonal educational plant replaced the old schoolhouse.

I have stopped in Enderupskov several times; it lies a day's journey from Roskilde and a few hours north of Kurt Schietzel's dig across the German border at Hedeby. On my first visit, I found Hartvig Nielsen in a pine forest a few miles from the village on a Sunday afternoon. He and his Boy Scouts were felling trees. "Timber for New Hedeby," he explained. "With Dr. Schietzel's cooperation, we're trying to build an exact duplicate of Hedeby."

We talked as we drove down to New Hedeby, on the Danish side of the border some 30 miles north of the original town. "Working rough material with one's own hands has always been part of scouting," Hartvig told me, "but the usual products were insignificant and even irrelevant. By immersing ourselves in the crafts of the Viking Age, we allow the boys to construct something of value.

"My initial idea was to copy a Viking ship. So some years ago, I called on an expert and asked for guidance in making a copy of the Ladby ship, the only Viking Age vessel unearthed in Denmark before the Roskilde finds. 'Don't waste your time with that!' he said. 'It can't sail!' At that time, the authorities believed that lack of a keel made the Ladby ship a nautical misfit.

"I argued that we were interested in the building techniques rather than the finished ship. Finally Mr. Crumlin-Pedersen agreed to advise us. We built the copy in the course of several years, using as precisely as possible the tools and procedures of the Vikings.

"And then we sailed it. To everyone's surprise, even our own, we found that —far from being unsailable—the Ladby ship must have been virtually unsinkable. With no keel, no part of the vessel bites into the water and offers resistance to heavy seas. The Ladby ship merely slides across the surface when buffeted by wind or wave. We've even transported horses and cattle without difficulty. Due solely to our experience, archeologists no longer laugh off the Ladby ship."

At the site of New Hedeby, Hartvig guided me through the ten buildings already constructed. Jammed together, with the inevitable planked roadway threading between, they had been built to an exact ground plan from Hedeby.

"As with the ship, we use only authentic tools," my guide continued. "Furthermore, the scouts cover all costs by contributing 40 cents for each day that they work here. So far, we've had 1,400 volunteers. And they learn history while they work.

"Our experience with the copy of the Ladby ship has underlined the skill of Viking shipwrights. Once a sizable fishing boat carried our crew of scouts to the island of Fyn to pick up the vessel. Every one of them became seasick. Coming back in our Ladby—across the same seas—there was no pitching, no rolling, just a gentle rocking. Nobody suffered a moment's discomfort.

"Another time we had a group of guests aboard. One, a professional mariner, had stationed himself forward and was lecturing to the others on the ship's characteristics. Suddenly a violent wind struck us. We were in mortal danger, but the ship's tilt was so gentle that the speaker never missed a phrase. Not until my son, manning the tiller, took an ax to the lines and collapsed the sail did anyone recognize the imminence of disaster. I assure you that there is no yacht afloat as seaworthy as that Viking-type craft.

"You may wonder why we've chosen the Viking Age for our projects. Well, the Vikings had a zest for life, a higher culture than we perhaps imagine, and certainly an artistic genius at working wood. And, as the boys learned on the Ladby ship, there was no special place for a chieftain—no bridge, no poop. Vikings sailed as equals, the leader assuming control only during crises.

"We're not just playing Viking, nor are we posing as doctors of archeology. Scouts are in a unique position to investigate the use of historic objects and methods. We're trying to make our contribution to knowledge."

Danish Boy Scout authorities, however—apparently considering the projects too great a departure from traditional scouting activities—have decided to foreclose Hartvig Nielsen's program. On my last visit I was told that New Hedeby will not be finished, that no new Viking ship replicas will be attempted.

But Hartvig will not be idle. Using the old tools and the old techniques, he is planning to build a copy of the Roskilde museum's knarr for the government of Canada, which hopes to moor it at L'Anse aux Meadows, site of a Norse settlement in Newfoundland. There is a possibility that a copy will also be ordered for the celebration of the United States bicentennial in 1976.

The arrival and exhibition of these vessels in the New World cannot help but inspire awe. Anyone who has seen the knarr at Roskilde has already experienced the feeling. A transatlantic packet only 54 feet long! I remembered the heaving, gunmetal-gray North Atlantic in winter, and wondered how any Viking vessel, any Norse sailor could have survived it. But survive it they did, and an unknown genius from the era of *Beowulf* fashioned a lyric monument to the mariners who endured hardship and loneliness, dolor and danger while battling the waves. The poem is *The Seafarer*; Ezra Pound has translated it from the Anglo-Saxon:

> *. . . Lest man know not*
> *That he on dry land loveliest liveth,*
> *List how I, care-wretched, on ice-cold sea,*
> *Weathered the winter, wretched outcast*
> *Deprived of my kinsmen;*
> *Hung with hard ice-flakes, where hail-scur flew,*
> *There I heard naught save the harsh sea*
> *And ice-cold wave, at whiles the swan cries,*
> *Did for my games the gannet's clamour,*
> *Sea-fowls' loudness was for me laughter,*
> *The mews' singing all my mead-drink.*
> *Storms, on the stone-cliffs beaten, fell on the stern*
> *In icy feathers; full oft the eagle screamed*
> *With spray on his pinion.*

Given such unremitting misery, why did men of that gnarled and merciless age follow the sea? The poet had an answer—one that rings of eternity, for a sailor could invoke it still:

> *He hath not heart for harping, nor in ring-having*
> *Nor winsomeness to wife, nor world's delight*
> *Nor any whit else save the wave's slash,*
> *Yet longing comes upon him to fare forth on the water.*
> *Bosque taketh blossom, cometh beauty of berries,*
> *Fields to fairness, land fares brisker,*
> *All this admonisheth man eager of mood,*
> *The heart turns to travel so that he then thinks*
> *On flood-ways to be far departing.*

And far, indeed, did the Norse depart. On a foggy morning, sometime after the year 800, a knarr nosed toward the high, wave-lashed Faeroe Islands. Commanding it was one Grim Kamban—Grim the Lame—a Norwegian Viking out of Ireland with family and livestock. No accident of navigation had brought

Grim's knarr to the Faeroes: He had come to find freedom and land. It is not improbable that he had learned of the islands' existence from Irish monks who, in search of solitude and salvation, had been sailing there in frail *currachs*, small boats made of skin stretched over a wooden frame, for more than a century.

In 825 the monk Dicuil described the Faeroes: "There are many other islands in the ocean to the north of Britain which can be reached from the northernmost British Isles in two days' and nights' direct sailing, with full sails and an undropping fair wind. . . . Some of these islands are very small; nearly all are separated one from the other by narrow sounds. On these islands hermits who have sailed from our Scotia [here, Ireland] have lived for roughly a hundred years. . . . I have never found these islands mentioned in the books of scholars."

Soon after Grim, others came—from the Hebrides and from Norway. They must have been men of substance, for Aud the Deep-Minded, widow of Olaf the White—a Viking magnate from Ireland—married her granddaughter to one of the settlers. There were several generations of liberty; then the Faeroes fell under Norwegian rule, and in 1380 passed to Denmark. In 1948, after more than 900 years as a subject people, the Faeroese regained internal self-government. Their parliament, the *Løgting*, convenes in the capital, Tórshavn, site of the *thing*-place of the early settlers; the first Faeroese althings met about the year 900.

In some respects the most isolated of extant Norse Atlantic colonies, the Faeroes have retained much of their Viking flavor: The population of 38,000 speaks a variant of Old Norse; most farm and fish for a living; the sea dominates their lives. The young men yearn for boats in the same way that their counterparts elsewhere yearn for high-performance sports cars. A Faeroese proverb declares, "A man without a boat is a man in chains."

I came to the islands—about 230 miles from the top of Scotland—by air. As we approached from the southeast, the ocean below lost its rich indigo hue; fading to zinc-gray, it seemed to reflect the subarctic skies. There is nothing gradual or graceful in the topography of the 18 islands of the lonely archipelago—no beaches, no gently curving bays. The cliffs rise from the waves as severe and forbidding as battlements. Indeed, throughout their history the Faeroes have been small fortresses under constant siege by a cold, unfriendly sea.

Sunny days occur rarely here; clouds crown every island height like bridal veils streaming in the northern winds. The moist climate—rainfall totals about 60 inches a year—does, however, create ideal conditions for raising sheep; thick green turf, almost luminescent in the wet air, covers hill and valley alike. As many as 70,000 of the animals roam the slopes, and Faeroese woolens have been an important export since early Viking times.

Trees, save for a few well-tended specimens in the larger towns, simply do not grow in the islands; thus the landscape has a stark and empty grandeur. Another result is that driftwood has always been highly prized, and men have even gone to court over its ownership—as they have over rights to catch seabirds and to gather seaweed.

The islanders' dependence upon the sea is all but complete: More than half the population engages in ocean-related occupations. Fish constitute 95

percent of exports; seafood, supplemented by mutton, forms the chief staple of diet. In these staunchly Lutheran islands the local sale of alcoholic beverages is banned. As a sop to sinners and a crutch to the weak, however, the law permits consumption of a singularly dismal product: nonalcoholic beer.

In the village of Kvívík on Streymoy, I paid my respects to a Faeroese patriarch, 92-year-old Graekaris Madsen. Fresh from a nap, Mr. Madsen received me in traditional attire: black knee breeches and black vest trimmed with silver buttons. He was interested to learn that I was an American; New York City, he said, owes the name of one of its boroughs, the Bronx, to a Faeroese, Jonas Bronck.

Mr. Madsen incarnates the long continuity of Faeroese culture, and the tenacity with which the islanders nurtured it during centuries of Danish domination. "When I was a boy," he told me, "we had no school in Kvívík. We'd never had one. My grandfather taught me to read and write and to obey the laws of God. He said, 'Honor thy father and thy mother, and all the ancestors from the very first to have settled here, and you will live long in the country.' That's what I've tried to do."

How, I asked, had he learned English?

"From a book that my family had. It was called *Teach Yourself English in 100 Hours*. I confess that it took me rather longer. Here in the Faeroes we have a proverb: 'Blind is the man without books.'

"My boyhood, I think, was typical. I fished as far away as Iceland. From time to time I farmed. Then, when I was 20, I shipped on an English trawler.

"When I was young, our biggest problem was to preserve our language and our heritage. The poets would purposely make their songs on Norwegian themes to keep people conscious that our heritage was Norwegian, not Danish.

And, even though the Danes banned all official use of our language, about 100 years ago the pastor in this village, Wenzel Hammershaimb, standardized Faeroese so that we could write it and print it."

Suddenly Mr. Madsen burst into song, his old man's voice squeaking on the high notes:

> *"Wenzel Hammershaimb prestur i Kvívík sjey ár. . . .*
> *Væl kendur av flestum føroyingum var,*
> *Og verdur, medan klettarnir standa."*

> *"Wenzel Hammershaimb, pastor in Kvívík seven years. . . .*
> *He was well known to most of the Faeroese people,*
> *And will be as long as the cliffs shall stand."*

As his voice died away, I realized that I had been listening to a living relic —a modern skaldic song. A millennium out of period, yet there it was: a verse composed in the last century to memorialize an important man's achievements.

Before leaving Kvívík I stopped at the farmstead, dating from approximately A.D. 1000, that has been excavated by Faeroese archeologist Sverri Dahl. Encroaching waves had long ago eroded the seaward ends of the two vestigial buildings. One had been a barn, and judging from the closeness of the stone partitions that separated the individual stalls, the cattle must have been small. The thick walls of the longhouse remained in truncated form, rising a foot and a half to four feet above the foundations. A long stone hearth occupied the middle of the house. Wooden posts once supported a roof of straw, birch bark, and turf. From scattered bones, Dahl infers that the Kvívík farmer and his family ate the meat of sheep, cows, pigs, seals, and pilot whales, as well as cod and seabirds.

The excavators found a solitary stone slab about two feet square beside the ember pit. Its purpose mystified them, but not Mr. Madsen, who had lent a hand in the dig. "Until the beginning of this century, all Faeroese spent the winter beside open fires," he explained. "And everyone had just such a slab beside his fire pit. We used it for drying stockings after fishing. I'm sure that the old Viking families did the same thing."

Erosion poses a continuing threat in the islands—from constant intrusions of the sea, from thousands of rain-swollen torrents that lacerate the green slopes, and above all from the grazing of sheep. "The maximum number we can support without destroying the land is 70,000," an official told me. "We slaughter 40,000 a year to keep the flocks within that figure."

I visited the Faeroes in mid-May, and I found that the islanders still observe a venerable Norse practice. To survive the coldest months, the flocks winter on the farmsteads of their owners; but on May 15 of every year, by law, they must be driven to summer pastures on the heights.

A passage from the 13th-century *Egil's Saga* explains the reason: "What livestock there was found its own food . . . through the winter. . . . all the sheep went up on the high ground for the summer. [Egil's father] could see a big difference, how the stock which went on the heath grew better and fatter. . . ."

In the lakes, ponds, and streams of the Faeroes thrive salmon and trout and arctic char. One cold, windy, and—inevitably—cloudy day, I joined Sigmund Petersen, president of the Anglers Association. Driving to northern Streymoy, we fished several lakes, and hiked up precipitous hills to high, secret ponds. Our luck was bad: Mr. Petersen caught three arctic char; I hooked one. But that day in the pure, cold northern air with the water clear and clean and the horizons vast and empty had a marvelous tonic effect.

While we were there, Mr. Petersen told me a story tragically illustrating the tension between man and the sea that overshadows all of Faeroese life.

"About 60 years ago," he said, "when I was a small boy, two fishing boats went down in a storm, drowning 14 men from two small neighboring villages. Of course, in those days the islands' population was much smaller, and everybody knew everybody else. I remembered how my mother cried and cried over those men. She wept for days, and I just couldn't understand why.

"Then I found out. The smaller of the villages, with a history that reached back almost to the time of the settlement, had simply ceased to exist. Its entire male population had been wiped out." Without their menfolk, he said, the families found it too difficult to continue, and moved to other communities.

In the evening, as we returned to Tórshavn from the long, frigid, glorious day in the hills, Mr. Petersen turned on the car radio to catch the news.

It was very grim. At four o'clock that afternoon, lashed by extreme winds, the Faeroese trawler *Sundaberg* with a crew of 38 and 450 tons of fish aboard had gone down at sea. We rode the rest of the way in deep gloom. Later we learned with great relief that a German vessel had responded to *Sundaberg*'s SOS and had picked up all the crew members from their storm-buffeted rubber rafts.

In the Faeroes, the sea gives and the sea takes away.

These fog-shrouded islands were little more than a way station on the Norse Atlantic odyssey of a thousand years ago. Probing ever westward, the knarrs of the colonizers reached Iceland around the year 870. The soil was fruitful, and settlers poured in. About 960 a quarrelsome man and his son Eric the Red, then a teen-ager, arrived in the new colony, having left their native Norway "because of some killings."

Against all odds, Eric made a brilliant marriage with the wealthy heiress Thjodhild and settled down on a fine farm. But the turbulent Norwegian soon slew two neighbors and involved himself in other difficulties. Iceland's Althing outlawed him for three years.

The bad-tempered bridegroom passed his banishment aboard a ship exploring a huge island to the west that had been sighted earlier by a Norse mariner. On the southwestern coast, Eric found pasture-fringed fjords, fertile valleys, and crystal streams. Sailing back to Iceland, he recruited a band of colonists. Volunteers abounded, not only because in Iceland the decent land was already taken up, but also because Eric had mounted a shrewd psychological gambit. Says his saga: "He called the country he had discovered Greenland, for he

*G*risly *bloodbath concludes a later Vinland voyage. Freydis, daughter*

of Eric the Red, had tricked her husband, Thorvard, into slaying

the men of one ship, secretly planning to take it over herself. When he

refused to kill the women, she took an ax and did the deed herself.

argued that men would be drawn to go there if the land had an attractive name."

Eric led a fleet of 25 ships back to his 840,000-square-mile island. The perils attending Viking voyagers in the North Atlantic may be measured by the fact that only 14 vessels arrived in Greenland.

The settlements established by Eric the Red in this essentially inhospitable land endured for five centuries. The colonists were Christianized in the 11th century, and in 1126 a bishop took up residence and presided over a spacious cathedral and a large episcopal farm. An Augustinian monastery and a Benedictine nunnery also thrived. By the year 1300, Norse Greenland numbered about 3,000 inhabitants on 300 farms.

The settlers had sunk their roots in two widely separated enclaves. The larger or Eastern Settlement curved just above Greenland's southernmost promontory, Cape Farewell. The more sparsely populated Western Settlement lay 400 miles to the northwest. From its highest mountains, on a good day, you could see the cloud bank that hovered above the North American coast.

Life on the Greenland farms must always have been marginal. Certain necessities depended upon the good will — or, more accurately, greed — of Norwegian merchant skippers. Only the arrival of their knarrs could bring the colonists desperately needed iron, timber, grain, and salt, plus the few luxuries that made life more pleasant.

The 13th-century Norwegian book, *The King's Mirror,* depicts the flow of Greenland trade: "Whatever comes from other lands is high in price, for this land lies so distant from other countries that men seldom visit it. And everything that is needed to improve the land must be purchased abroad, both iron and all the timber used in building houses. In return for their wares the merchants bring back the following products: buckskin, or hides, sealskins, and rope . . . which is called 'leather rope' and is cut from the fish called walrus, and also the teeth of the walrus."

Hunting these commodities imposed severe hardships on the colonists. In 1824, an Eskimo found a 14th-century runestone on the Greenland coast more than 6° north of the Arctic Circle. Flat and black, broken off at a length of less than five inches, it says: "Saturday before the minor Rogation Day [April 25], Erling Sigvatson and Bjarne Thordarson and Einride Oddson erected these cairns and . . ." Clearly these hunters, who had quested 900 miles north of Cape Farewell in search of the game that spelled survival for Norse Greenland, had been forced to winter there. The ruins of a hut for such a stay have been found near Disko Island, about 150 miles south.

As early as 1267 the Eskimos — whom the settlers called Skraelings, the term they used for all the natives they encountered in the New World — appeared on the northwestern coast of Greenland, but there is little evidence that they were hostile. Nevertheless, toward the middle of the 14th century the colonies began to decline. Communication between the two settlements, never frequent, tailed off. In the face of a long silence, a certain Ivar Bardarson took part in an expedition from the Eastern Settlement to contact the Western. One account of his trip,

in an old English version, does violence to orthography but dramatically conveys the devastation that he found: "All this before Written was done by one Iver Boty [Bardarson] borne in Gronland, a principall man in the Bishop's Court: who dwelt there many yeeres, and saw and knew all these places. He was chosen by the whole Land for Captayne, to goe with Ships to the Westland, to drive away their Enemies the Skerlengers [Skraelings]. But hee comming there, found no people neither Christian nor Heathen, but found there many Sheepe running being wilde, of which Sheepe they took with them as many as they could carrie, and with them returned to there Houses."

So, on a note of mystery, ended the Western Settlement. And the farmers in the Eastern Settlement in time began to clash with the Eskimos. The Icelandic annals from 1379 inform us that "the Skraelings made a raid on the Greenlanders, killing 18 men and carrying off two boys as slaves."

The last literary source mentioning Greenland dates from 1410. In the Icelandic annals, four men affirm "that in the year of Our Lord one thousand four hundred and eight we were present in Hvalsey church, in Greenland, on the Sunday after the Exaltation of the Cross and witnessed the wedding of Sigrid Bjornsdatter and Thorstein Olafson."

After that, silence.

Beginning in 1585, Englishman John Davis sailed three times to southwestern Greenland. He found only Eskimos. The fate of the Norse colonies remains a mystery. When merchant ships ceased to sail there — as they did some time in the 14th century — did the Greenlanders die slowly of deprivation? Did the Black Death, arriving from a stricken Europe on some random vessel, exterminate them? In desperation did they depart for the richer lands of America? Did the Skraelings destroy them?

No one can answer. Archeologists are confident that the key lies somewhere in the ruins of the Greenland farmsteads, and that one day they will unearth it.

Meanwhile, one tantalizing clue exists. German and English pirates raided repeatedly in Iceland in the 15th century, and an extension of their activities to Greenland would have been logical. Niels Egede, son of a missionary sent by the Danish government, grew up on the great, frozen island in the early 18th century. From an Eskimo shaman living among the ruins of the Eastern Settlement, he recorded a curious folk tale passed down through the shaman's forefathers. It recounted how the Eskimos and Norse had lived in uneasy proximity until, presumably in the 15th century, the arrival of sinister strangers. "Three small ships came sailing in from the southwest to plunder, and some of the Norwegians were killed . . ." goes the old Eskimo tale. "The next year a whole fleet arrived and fought with them, plundering and killing. . . . The year after that the dreadful pirates came back once again, and when we saw them we fled, taking some of the Norwegian women and children with us up the fjord, and left the others. . . . When we returned in the autumn hoping to find some people again, we saw to our horror that everything had been carried away, and houses and farms were burned down. . . . At this sight we took the women and children back with us and fled far up the fjord, and we stayed there in peace and quiet for many years. We married the Norwegian women — there were only five of them with some children — and when we finally grew to be many, we left there and settled up and down the country."

I reached Greenland in the dark hush of winter. The air was very still and frigid — the temperature far below zero — and the brittle snow crackled underfoot. Elongated shadows that would linger until the vernal equinox enshrouded the snowscape in a permanent, ominous twilight. I wondered how those men of long ago had ever endured this annual ordeal by frost. At Cape Farewell, great slabs of ice clog the sea. They float with the current like huge, misshapen cenotaphs, eternal memorials to the doomed Vikings who dared this arctic desolation — and lost.

The Greenland colony ended in mystery and tragedy, but its early days provided the world with a momentous and largely ignored discovery.

Sailing from Norway to Greenland in 986, Bjarni Herjulfsson was blown past his destination by unfavorable winds. For five days he and his crew paralleled the coast of North America, but did not land. Later, when Bjarni told his story, "people thought how lacking in enterprise and curiosity he had been." But his tale awakened new land-lust in Greenland, and Leif, son of Eric the Red, bought Bjarni's ship and prepared to explore westward. Leif, we are told, "was big and strong, of striking appearance, shrewd, and in every respect a temperate, fair-dealing man."

Two literary sources—*Eric the Red's Saga* and *The Greenlanders' Saga*—record Leif's voyage of discovery and the ill-starred Norse attempts to colonize North America. Sailing about the year 1000, Leif followed Bjarni's course in reverse. He came first to a forbidding mass of mountains and glaciers which he named *Helluland*, or Flatstone Land. Then he sailed south and went ashore on a sandy beach with woodlands beyond, which he called *Markland*, Forestland. Farther south still, he and his crew came upon a place "so choice, it seemed to them that none of the cattle would require fodder for the winter." They found "salmon there in river and lake . . . bigger than they had ever seen before," and later vines and grapes as well.

Leif built a house and spent the winter. He called his discovery *Vinland*, or Wineland. Virtually all scholars now agree that Helluland was Baffin Island, and Markland was Labrador. Leif's Vinland settlement remains unidentified, but most think it was somewhere in Newfoundland.

Subsequently, another son of Eric, Thorvald, explored the new continent even farther. At a certain headland, he and his party "brought the ship to where they could moor her, thrust out a gangway to the shore, and Thorvald walked ashore with his full ship's company. 'This is a lovely place,' he said, 'and here I should like to make my home.' Then they made for the ship, and saw three mounds on the sands up inside the headland. They walked up to them and could see three skin-boats there, and three men under each. So they divided forces and laid hands on them all, except for one who got away with his canoe. The other eight they killed, and afterwards walked back to the headland, where they had a good look round and could see various mounds on up the fjord which they judged to be human habitations."

But Thorvald had blundered fatally by killing the eight Skraelings. The survivor sounded the alarm, and the Indians in "a countless fleet of skin-boats" attacked the Norsemen. An arrow dispatched the luckless Thorvald. With a fine irony, he was buried on that headland he had hoped "to make my home."

The Greenlanders mounted at least one major effort to colonize Vinland. Early in the 11th century, according to Eric the Red's saga, Thorfinn Karlsefni fitted out three ships, loaded them with 160 men and women and sufficient livestock, and sailed to a place in North America that he named Straumfjord. His colony prospered for three years—during which time Thorfinn's wife gave birth to the first white child born in America, a boy named Snorri—but again trouble developed with the Skraelings, culminating in a pitched battle. At the end of the third winter, Thorfinn gave up the struggle and sailed back to Greenland.

Nevertheless, other voyagers made American landfalls for centuries to come. The Icelandic annals for 1121 record that "Bishop Eirik of Greenland went in search of Vinland." And in 1347, "There came also a ship from Greenland. . . . There were 17 men on board. They had made a voyage to Markland, but were afterwards storm-driven here."

After centuries of speculation regarding the veracity of the saga accounts of Vinland, Norwegian scholar Helge Ingstad vindicated them when, in 1962, he discovered the remains of a Viking settlement at L'Anse aux Meadows near

Sun-tinged foam washes the shore beneath the basalt cliffs

of Dyrhólaey. Towering 500 feet, the headland gave Viking

colonists their first glimpse of southern Iceland.

the northern tip of Newfoundland. Carbon-14 testing of organic material found on the site dates the settlement at approximately A.D. 1000.

Mr. Ingstad and his wife, Anne Stine, an archeologist, spent eight years excavating at L'Anse aux Meadows. Objects of metal and wood disintegrate rapidly in the acid soil, but the Ingstads have found a whetstone for sharpening needles, a spindle whorl, and a bronze pin—all obviously of Viking origin.

When I visited L'Anse aux Meadows, I found that the "choice" land of the sagas remains so still. The old settlement lies beside an ellipse of beach protected by headlands and islands. Berries, scarlet and dusty blue, carpet the springy earth. A stream of cold, swift water, darkened and made tangy by its high iron content, winds down into the bay. Salmon lurk in the shade of its banks and once, as I rounded a bend, a huge trout leaped convulsively.

Southerly winds temper the climate. Winters are short and relatively mild, summers a long dream of quivering green as the breeze ruffles the junipers and laurels.

Ten Newfoundland families inhabit the tiny hamlet of L'Anse aux Meadows, hard by the Viking site. And they live not unlike the old Norsemen. They keep cattle and sheep—and the pasture does indeed last through the winter. Chickens peck in their dooryards. With the seasons, they take trout in the streams and seals in the bay. In the autumn they hunt for ducks and, whenever the opportunity arises, they poach a few lobsters. And, as one man told me, they like their way of life "wonderful well."

With Mr. Ingstad, I walked among the excavated relics of the Viking settlement—past the smithy with its scattering of 1,000-year-old charcoal, past the trenches streaked with the dark brown, time-compressed layers of turf that had formed the walls of the longhouses, dwellings virtually indistinguishable from the Faeroese farmhouse I had seen at Kvívík. Green moss creeps inexorably across the trodden earth floors, engulfing the cooking and storage pits and even the great central hearths. A sizable group—certainly no smaller than Thorfinn's—had occupied this site. Regular, tapering concavities in the sod of a small shelf just above the beach showed where they had built sheds for their small boats. The knarrs had probably remained at anchor in the bay.

"Why did the colony fail?" Mr. Ingstad echoed my question. "It failed simply because the weapons of the Vikings were no better than the weapons of the Skraelings, and the Skraelings far outnumbered the Norse settlers. Columbus succeeded, I think, largely because he had firearms."

Flock of Icelandic sheep moves from highland pastures above the village of Flúdir. During an autumn roundup, mounted shepherds and dogs like the one below herd more than half a million sheep into coastal corrals for shearing or for slaughter. In the Viking Age, Icelandic farmers prospered by shipping sheepskins and woolen cloth to Norway.

BOTH THOMAS NEBBIA

Seizing head and tail, villagers of Stafn in northern Iceland corral a pony for sale. Below, young riders—tousled and rosy-cheeked after a gallop—share a horse descended from stock that has ranged the island for 1,100 years. In this early period, the sagas say, many people in Norse countries enjoyed horse fights between trained stallions.

Althing, an Icelandic assembly of free men, gives audience to a father (in red cape) wh

as just announced his daughter's divorce. Viking wives could leave their husbands at will.

*S*himmering Öxará River tumbles through a volcanic gorge into
Lake Thingvellir, on whose shore Iceland's first Althing
        met. The scarcity of timber forced the Norse settlers to build
dwellings of sod and rock. A cluster of houses on present-day Glaumbaer
Farm in northern Iceland resembles a ninth-century settlement.

*P*lunging his flensing knife deep, an Icelander carves blubber at a whaling station nea

Reykjavik. Norse hunters found whales plentiful here and feasted on their steaks.

Jakobshavn Glacier looms above a kayaker on the west coast of

Greenland, first visited by Eric the Red in 982. Exiled from Iceland

for manslaughter, Eric spent three years exploring Greenland's

coastline. On his return home, he induced settlers to join him

in colonizing the head of Eiriks Fjord. There they founded Brattahlid,

where the stone foundation of an early 14th-century

church still stands (below). When the late Middle Ages came to an

end, Norse colonies in Greenland had mysteriously disappeared.

Gudrid, wife of Thorfinn Karlsefni, dresses their son Snorri—the first European born in Nort

merica—in 11th-century Vinland. The Karlsefni group of settlers remained just three years.

*D*arkness settles over Newfoundland as fisherman Lloyd Decker gazes out to sea from L'Anse aux Meadows. In 1961, Norwegian archeologist Helge Ingstad and his wife, Anne Stine, began to excavate this Viking community that dates to about A.D. 1000. Their digging has unearthed seven houses, a smithy, four boat sheds, a charcoal kiln, and two cooking pits. Near the site, a fisherman's son carries dried codfish; other children pick wild berries.

unning before the wind, the knarrs of colonization spread Norse settlements throughout the North Atlantic. But the seizure of new territory did nothing to abate the carnage in Europe. Even as farmers were harvesting their first crops in the Faeroes, repeated assaults by their cousins brought one of France's fairest provinces, Neustria, to the brink of ruin. The easily-navigable Seine River, which roughly bisected Neustria, flowed from the heart of France through Paris and past Rouen. Between Rouen and the English Channel, wealthy monasteries such as Jumièges and St.-Wandrille drowsed among their fields and orchards.

To these monasteries the dragon ships brought doom. A history of the monastery of St.-Wandrille de Fontenelle, founded in 649, relates how the Vikings first arrived in 841. "At dawn on 13 May, the monks . . . watched with stupefaction" as the first longships they had ever seen sailed silently upriver. The Northmen captured Rouen, pillaged and burned for two days, and returned, "amusing themselves by sacking churches and abbeys."

In January, 852, another band of Vikings swept up the river channel. This time they burned St.-Wandrille and leveled all its buildings. Another fleet arrived in October. By 858 the repeated hammerblows of the Danish raiders proved too much for the monks. With the relics of their saints, they fled. Not for 102 years—by which time Neustria had been transformed into a Viking duchy and the Vikings, in turn, had been transformed into Christians—did they return.

Of all the monasteries along the Seine that suffered Viking attacks, only St.-Wandrille has survived. The abbey lies beside the narrow, limpid Fontenelle River about a mile above its junction with the north bank of the Seine. In that high green valley, men have been following the austere rule of St. Benedict— save when interrupted by Vikings or French revolutionaries—for more than a thousand years. I spent a day with the monks of St.-Wandrille in their world that knows neither yesterday nor tomorrow, but only Eternity. They rose in the chill darkness of 5 a.m., and 5:20 found all 50 of them assembled in the starkly beautiful church for Matins. Seven times in the course of the day they sang the divine office in the stately cadences of Gregorian chant. The bells of the abbey punctuated the hours.

"Here at St.-Wandrille," said Dom Joseph Thiron, the spare, precise sub-prior, "we pass our time between prayer and work. The regimen is all balance, all routine. It is, I assure you, a most delightful life. But one with different values. For example, to pray effectively we must maintain an atmosphere of quiet. In your world, it is only civil to exchange a word with your fellows. Here, the civility is silence."

Dom Joseph showed me through the enclosed 30 acres of gardens and cloisters and chapels, including a small factory that processes wax into floor polish. "It is a good product," said the subprior, "and an important source of income to the monastery."

Every monk spends a part of each day on the modest assembly line; when I

NORMANS

*S*unlight burnishes the sepulcher of Hrolf the Ganger (Rollo),
first Duke of Normandy, in Notre-Dame Cathedral at Rouen.

passed by, the abbot—his sleeves tucked up—was clamping tops on filled cans.

Within a Benedictine monastery, the rule of the abbot is virtually absolute. Does the assignment of tasks, I asked Dom Joseph, ever give rise to resentment?

"Not really. A good abbot respects the competencies and tastes of his monks. After all, one doesn't put a deaf man in charge of the organ."

Two plain meals a day are served in a refectory of simplicity and surpassing beauty. At the head of the hall, beneath a crucifix on the otherwise bare stone wall, the abbot sits alone. On either side, tables line the huge room and the monks occupy them in order of descending age. For dinner we had fish, potatoes, cheese, and bread. Visitors were served a pitcher of excellent Norman cider; the monks drank water.

I left St.-Wandrille after dark. The lights of the church shone warm and golden through the winter night, and faintly I could hear the voices of the monks singing their last office of the day, Compline. As I wound down toward the fog-shrouded bottomlands of the Seine, the chant seemed to follow me—an anthem that for long centuries has sustained men of faith in this battered redoubt of God's kingdom.

By the year 900, little plunder remained in Neustria. Everywhere monks had fled their abbeys; abandoned farms decayed amid untended fields. Nonetheless, a Danish army headed by a Norse outlaw called Gangr Hrolf—Hrolf the Ganger, or Walker—spent the first decade of the tenth century gleaning what was left in the Seine Valley. Hrolf—known to French history as Rollo—won his cognomen, the Walker, because no ordinary horse could carry him. Friendly chroniclers claimed that he was too tall; the unfriendly ones maintained that he was too fat.

In 911, the Frankish King Charles the Simple—who was anything but simple—purchased peace with the ultimate danegeld: To Hrolf he ceded as a dukedom all of Neustria that his Vikings held, provided he would embrace Christianity and defend his new duchy against other northern raiders. Hrolf pledged fealty to Charles in 912, and received the sacrament of baptism; many of his followers also became Christians.

The Vikings wore their new religion lightly, however. Some sought baptism as often as 20 times for the sake of the white garments given to converts. And when Hrolf died, his requiem service proved that he had not forgotten Thor. In addition to large donations to monasteries for masses to be sung for his soul's repose, he had ordered the sacrifice of 100 prisoners.

The Franks had known the former raiders as *Nordmanni*, or Northmen, and the label passed to their new homeland in the form of Normandy.

At about the same time Charles the Simple was presenting Neustria to Hrolf, he rid himself of another pestilence of pirates by ceding to the Loire Vikings all the territory in the vicinity of Nantes. But the Northmen of the Loire had no dominant figure such as Hrolf. The new barons fell to squabbling among themselves—ever a notable Viking characteristic—and by 937 had lost the Nantois duchy by default.

Unlike their fellow Scandinavians in Kiev, the Vikings of Normandy did not simply disappear into their new surroundings. Rather, they combined with the native French population to produce a unique people of hardihood and genius destined to dominate the affairs of Europe for more than a century. Before their epoch of glory ended, the Normans ruled in Britain and southern Italy and Sicily; they commanded principalities as far afield as Antioch and Jerusalem. Rome fell to them, popes implored their aid, and their fleets controlled the Mediterranean. But in the end, they lost it all; for Norman empires had the diamond glitter and the sad evanescence of morning dew.

In Normandy itself, I wondered, did the Vikings leave any permanent imprint? To obtain an answer, I sought out a distinguished philologist who was then provost of one of the finest high schools in France, the *Lycée Malherbe* in the Norman city of Caen. M. Fernand Lechanteur, a man who had taken up arms under General Charles de Gaulle to fight for French freedom during World War II, spent a long afternoon with me discussing Scandinavian influences throughout Normandy.

"Our bond with the North," he declared, "reveals itself most clearly in place names and family names. Take the latter: In Normandy we now have a famous champion bicycle racer, Jacques Anquetil; the Scandinavian original is Arnketil. Toustain and Toutain, both common Norman family names, derive from the Norse Thorstein.

"I've just finished a study of place names in Normandy and, frankly, the Norse penetration in intra-village terminology astounded me. Let me first make a comparison. In eastern France, which has changed hands between this country and Germany for centuries, many cities and villages bear German names— Strasbourg, for instance, or Metz. In the names of such towns you can find the echo of the ancient fief. But most of the internal appellations, of streets and landmarks, are French. In Normandy, this is not so.

"The town names—and an incredible number of them, such as Quettehou and Houlgate, are pure Norse—represent only the beginning. Every coastal village has its big rock called *le holm;* every inland hamlet calls its clump of trees *londe*, from *lundr*, the Old Norse word for grove; the highest point of a village is always *hogue*, from *haugr*, Old Norse for hill.

"Presently in Normandy, scholars dispute whether the Viking settlers were few or many; the current fashion is to call them few and to minimize their influence. I cannot accept this. All of the philological evidence indicates that Northmen pervaded Normandy; their linguistic traces are everywhere.

"As for the psychology of us Normans, how can I express it? We are French, of course—that above all—but we also consider ourselves men of the North. We're proud of our Scandinavian heritage, and proud too of our contributions to the world. Not the least of these is England, which has borne a Norman hallmark since 1066."

That hallmark was stamped by a lineal descendant of Hrolf the Ganger who was born out of wedlock. He began his career as William the Bastard; he ended it having gained immortality as William the Conqueror.

Viking mercenary Harald Hardraada disputes the choice of a campsite with Georgios Maniakes, his commander on Sicily. Hardraada cheated the general in drawing lots for the site, and continued to defy him during the ill-fated Greek attempt to conquer the island.

The story of an episode of his early life, though perhaps apocryphal, illuminates his forceful character. Partly because of the endemic rebelliousness of Norman barons, the young William had been forced to fight hard to hold his duchy. Once he secured his title, he requested the hand of Matilda of Flanders, a pretty cousin, in marriage. She snapped: "I would rather be a veiled nun than be given to a bastard."

William swallowed the insult. But his resentment intensified until one day he rode wildly to the palace of the Duke of Flanders at Lisle. Pushing his way into Matilda's chambers, he seized the proud girl by the hair, dragged her across the floor, and kicked her savagely. Then he galloped back to his duchy.

Smitten with a sudden respect for her illegitimate cousin, and perhaps even with love, Matilda agreed to the marriage. It was a fortunate match. To the bewilderment of his biographers, William proved a thoroughly faithful husband; and Matilda's coronation as Queen of England in 1068 vindicated the choice of William as her liege lord.

The apogee of William's life, and a pivotal point in world history, came with his conquest of England in 1066. Even geography was jarred by the magnitude of this event. The ever-enlarging role of the Danes in England in the tenth century, the victories of Svein Forkbeard, and the reign of Knut the Great had conspired to sweep the British Isles into the northern orbit. By the middle of the 11th century, most of Europe regarded England as Scandinavian. Northmen considered the annexation a *fait accompli*. For two centuries they had maintained colonies there; as for the future, both Harald Hardraada of Norway and Svein Estridsson of Denmark had claims to the English throne.

But so did William. A swift, brilliantly executed campaign of conquest won him the crown. Ironically, inasmuch as he himself was of Viking descent, his feat wrenched the British Isles back into western Europe. Culturally and politically, they have remained there ever since.

A vivid pictorial account of William's exploit has been preserved on a roll of linen, 231 feet long and 20 inches wide, known as the Bayeux Tapestry. Evidence suggests that the Conqueror's half-brother Odo, Bishop of Bayeux—a decidedly uncanonical prelate who wielded a mace in William's host—commissioned English seamstresses to embroider what could be described as the first documentary film. Almost certainly, Odo and his episcopal successors unfurled it on festive occasions in the chancel of Bayeux's Cathedral of Notre-Dame. Now exhibited under glass in the former bishop's palace, just across the street from the cathedral, the tapestry affords not only a dramatic account of the Norman Conquest but also unrivaled glimpses into the everyday life of the time. We see, for example, a Norman farmer working his field with a donkey-drawn plow, and a hunter closing in on a boar with drawn sword. Troops in the field use their shields as mess kits; William and his retinue sip wine from drinking horns.

We see William building his invasion fleet; his shipwrights employ Scandinavian techniques, and the fearsome dragon heads of yore grace the prows of the vessels. But the scenes depicting the provisioning of the ships indicate how fundamentally the Normans had succumbed to French influence: They load neither ale nor mead, but rather huge casks of wine.

The panels portraying the Norman arrival in England have a sickening familiarity. Ruthlessly the invaders requisitioned food, stripping farms of livestock and stores. They put houses to the torch and created instant refugees.

The climactic battle at Hastings unfolds phase by phase. The Norman cavalry charges the Saxon shield-wall; a feigned retreat draws the English infantry in pursuit; the Normans turn and annihilate them. Harold Godwinson, the English king, takes an arrow in the eye and dies. On a final, grisly note of realism, we see the looting of the corpses. In the end, the fallen of both victors and vanquished lie naked and desolate on the battlefield.

On Christmas Day of 1066, in Westminster Abbey, the Archbishops of

York and Canterbury placed the crown of England upon William's head. He ruled firmly, bringing security and justice to the shires. Treason was put down with a swift and heavy hand. When York rose against him in 1069, he devastated the region so thoroughly that the land lay derelict for a generation. He invaded both Scotland and Wales on vengeful missions of reprisal.

After his death in 1087, the Anglo-Saxon Chronicle hazarded an evaluation of his character: "King William . . . was a man of great wisdom and power, and surpassed in honour and in strength all those who had gone before him. Though stern beyond measure to those who opposed his will, he was kind to those good men who loved God. . . . Among other things we must not forget the good order he kept in the land, so that a man of any substance could travel unmolested throughout the country with his bosom full of gold. . . . Assuredly in his time men suffered grievous oppression and manifold injuries. . . . He was sunk in greed and utterly given up to avarice. . . . May Almighty God shew mercy to his soul and pardon him his sins."

Normandy cherishes the memory of the Conqueror. In Caen, you can visit the impressive Abbaye aux Hommes built by William in return for a papal dispensation allowing him to marry his cousin Matilda. The old church at Dives-sur-Mer, his port of embarkation, displays a list of his companions chiseled into the stone wall. And the castle of his birth at Falaise has become a tourist attraction.

But this Viking duchy also produced another dynasty—one that bedazzled both the Christian and the Moslem worlds. I found its only memorial in a virtually uncharted village of the Cotentin Peninsula of northwestern France. You must be persistent to find Hauteville-la-Guichard, with its single church, its single cafe, and its population of 463.

I arrived there on an April day that was typical of December, and the temperature hovered just above freezing. Like uncertain offspring clinging to the skirts of a mother, the buildings of the village cluster around the churchyard. As I walked through the cemetery that surrounds the 11th-century church, a vicious wind cuffed funeral wreaths among the graves like tumbleweeds and caused bronze crucifixes to chatter against their mountings.

Trying door after door, I finally found one unlocked, and entered the church. I stepped into sudden quiet; the echoes of my footsteps rang against the walls. On the right of the chancel, amid the stations of the cross, I found the modest marble plaque I sought:

> To the memory of Tancred de Hauteville, of Mureille and Fressende, his two wives, of William Iron-Arm, Drogo, Humphrey, Geoffrey, and Serlon, Robert Guiscard, Mauger, William, Auvray, Tancred, Humbert and Roger, their twelve sons, and of their descendants conquerors of Apulia, of Calabria and of Sicily. Founders of the Norman Kingdom of Sicily. Ancestors of several reigning dynasties of Europe.
>
> 1035-1194
>
> They conquered the Eastern Emperor and the Holy Roman Emperor, re-established Pope Gregory VII in Rome, liberated from the Moslems a part

of the littoral of Africa, dominated the Adriatic and the Mediterranean, introduced in Sicily a remarkable political regime and a brilliant civilization, wisely governed and pacified their peoples.

The most incredible aspect of this inscription is that it is true. From this bleak agricultural hamlet, from the loins of a near-impoverished landowner, came an array of sons of such valor and such vigor that they bestrode their age.

As I stood in the cold, austere northern church, I experienced an ache of nostalgia for those lands of the south. For I had already visited Apulia and Calabria and Sicily, the scenes of the Hauteville conquests, and I remembered the orange trees in the Norman cloisters of Palermo; the cathedral of Cefalù, built by Tancred's grandson, embowered in blue sea and green palms; the soft rains of winter; the summer sun, a daze of brightness.

A century ago John Addington Symonds wrote: "No chapter of history more resembles a romance than that which records the sudden rise and brief splendour of the house of Hauteville. In one generation the sons of Tancred passed from the condition of squires in the Norman vale of Cotentin, to kinghood in the richest island of the southern sea. The Norse adventurers became Sultans of an Oriental capital. The sea-robbers assumed together with the sceptre the culture of an Arabian court."

History does, indeed, repeat itself. Vikings had seized Normandy because they lacked property at home in Scandinavia. Now, equally deprived in their new homeland, younger sons looked beyond the borders. "The people had increased so exceedingly that the fields and forests were no longer sufficient to provide for them," observed a historian of the Normans, Amatus of Monte Cassino, "and so these men departed, forsaking what was meagre in search of what was plentiful." Their acquisitive eyes focused upon southern Italy, a land invitingly wracked by chaos. Part of the Byzantine Empire since the sixth century, Greek in spirit and religion, the Italian provinces bore the name *Magna Graecia*, or Great Greece. Latin Lombards, however, mounted rebellion upon rebellion, and self-created local counts—more properly warlords—preyed upon Greeks, Lombards, and each other. In such a setting, an astute knight might even emulate the great Hrolf.

So, early in the 11th century, with weapons, mounts, and little else, Norman knights began drifting down the peninsula. Eager and hardy mercenaries, they fought for anyone willing to meet their price.

In 1030 the Duke of Naples felt the need for a reliable company of knights close at hand. So he settled the modest town of Aversa, with its territories, upon one of the Norman leaders named Rainulf in exchange for martial services. Sometime around 1035, the three eldest sons of Tancred de Hauteville—William and Drogo and Humphrey—arrived in Aversa and took service with Rainulf.

Not far away, separated from the toe of the Italian boot by the Strait of Messina, lay the largest—and potentially the richest—island in the Mediterranean: Sicily. Once a Byzantine possession, the island had crumbled in the ninth century before the tidal wave of Islam. From abundant riches and power in the Greek world of the fifth century B.C., Sicily *(Continued on page 156)*

Its cliffs and cathedral dominate Cefalù, a Sicilian port captured by

the Normans in the 11th century. On the Plain of Maniakes (below),

Norman mercenaries helped a Greek force rout the Saracens in 1038.

Later, under Norman rule, cultures fused in Sicily; in the cloisters

of the Monreale Cathedral near Palermo, Byzantine influence appears in

the mosaics, Greek in the column capitals, Moslem in the pointed arches.

Leaf wrappings protect their horses as cavalrymen led by William Bras-de-Fer (leaning i

saddle) and blond Hardraada prepare to charge through broken pottery scattered by the Saracens.

had slid into poverty under the misrule of the Romans and their successors.

Almost 200 years of Saracen rule changed, but did not notably enrich, the island. The Moslems introduced the cultivation of lemons and bitter oranges; they grew sugarcane and refined it; they planted date palms, pistachios, melons. Under their aegis Palermo, with its population of 100,000, became larger than any city in Christendom save Constantinople.

But by 1038 the Byzantine emperor, Michael IV, yearned to win Sicily back to the true faith and the imperial crown. He entrusted the mission to his greatest general, Georgios Maniakes. A huge man, Maniakes had a countenance "neither gentle nor pleasing, but put one in mind of a tempest . . . his hands seemed made for tearing down walls or for smashing doors of bronze."

Spearheading Maniakes's vast army was the Varangian Guard, commanded at that time by the young, ambitious, and—like the general—very tall Harald Hardraada. To add even greater strength, the Greek general recruited a detachment of 300 Norman knights from Aversa. Among them were William and Drogo de Hauteville. When Maniakes led his men ashore on Sicily, success followed success: Messina fell, and so did Rometta. Before the walls of Syracuse, young William de Hauteville rode down the city's emir and slew him, winning the name Bras-de-Fer, or Iron-Arm.

Near the western slope of Mount Etna the Greek forces met sharp resistance but finally prevailed; the battlefield to this day is known as Campo di Maniaci, the Plain of Maniakes. Costly as it was, the victory brought all of eastern Sicily under the Greeks' control, within two years of their arrival.

Then Maniakes's luck abruptly changed. He antagonized the Normans, and they departed for Italy. Then, in a justifiable rage, he struck the Byzantine admiral, a thoroughly inept commander but—unfortunately for the violent general—a brother-in-law of the emperor. Michael IV recalled Maniakes to Constantinople in disgrace and locked him in irons. The Greek reconquest, so promisingly begun, ended in disaster and retreat.

But the reputation won on the fields of Sicily by the Norman William Bras-de-Fer served him well. Once more on the mainland, he and his brothers rallied to the Lombard standard in Apulia and attacked the Greeks, their erstwhile employers. By 1042 the Normans had crushed the Byzantines, and William's comrades—now the most powerful force in the province—acclaimed him as the Count of Apulia.

William died young, probably in 1046, and his brother Drogo succeeded to the Apulian title. About this time, several more Normans crossed the Alps into Italy. Among them was Robert de Hauteville, who would soon win the name Guiscard, best translated as the Cunning One. Drogo assigned him to command of a garrison in the barren and impoverished hills of Calabria. There Robert had to steal food and horses to maintain his modest troop; on at least one occasion, he raised cash by kidnaping a Greek official. But Guiscard, a towering, rollicking man, possessed both genius and ambition; gradually he won control of troubled Calabria and the adjoining territories. Upon the deaths of his brothers he succeeded to Drogo's holdings in Apulia and Humphrey's near Salerno.

To the papacy, deeply embroiled in European politics, the newly established Norman overlords of southern Italy appeared as a God-given counterbalance to the German rulers of the Holy Roman Empire who periodically sought to impose their hegemony south of the Alps. So, in 1059, Pope Nicholas II and the Norman adventurers reached an agreement: In return for papal recognition of their conquests, the Normans would defend the popes against the Germans. At the Apulian town of Melfi, Robert knelt before Nicholas II to be invested as Duke of Apulia and of Calabria. Hoping to seduce him into driving the infidel from Sicily, the Pope also made him "by the Grace of God and of St. Peter . . . future Duke of Sicily."

Anna Comnena, whose father the Emperor Alexius bore the brunt of Robert Guiscard's subsequent thrusts at Byzantium, described the dashing brigand with a mixture of fascination and distaste. "This Robert," she wrote, "was Norman by descent, of insignificant origin, in temper tyrannical, in mind most cunning, brave in action, very clever in attacking the wealth and substance of magnates, most obstinate in achievement. . . . His stature was so lofty that he surpassed even the tallest, his complexion was ruddy, his hair flaxen, his shoulders were broad, his eyes all but emitted sparks of fire. . . . Thus equipped by fortune, physique and character, he was naturally indomitable, and subordinate to nobody in the world. Powerful natures are ever like this, people say, even though they be of somewhat obscure descent."

Cloaked in his new legitimacy, Guiscard continued to campaign up and down the peninsula, taming his ever-refractory barons and enlarging his dominions. One of his greater satisfactions came when he broke the power of his hated brother-in-law Gisulf, the Lombard Prince of Salerno. Confined to the citadel of his city, Gisulf withstood Robert's siege engines for almost a year, but in the end sued for terms. Guiscard promised to allow Gisulf and his followers to depart in peace on two conditions: that he surrender title to all his territories, and that he also turn over Salerno's holiest relic, a tooth of St. Matthew. The prince, who had prudently secreted this revered object in the citadel, was as determined to keep it as Guiscard was to acquire it.

He agreed to Robert's terms without hesitation; then, showing a nice concern for authenticity of a sort, he ordered that a tooth be drawn from the jaw of a hapless Jew in his retinue. This he wrapped with rich cloth and sent to his brother-in-law. But the Cunning One summoned a priest familiar with the holy object, who at once pronounced the substitute a fraud. Thereupon Robert informed Gisulf that if the true tooth were not turned over, he would regretfully be forced to extract all of the prince's own. Gisulf surrendered the holy molar and, stripped of relic and principality, sullenly rode away.

For his part, Guiscard promptly proclaimed Salerno—the largest city in Italy south of Rome—his new capital, and built a magnificent cathedral to house the relic of St. Matthew.

The title to Sicily granted him by Pope Nicholas II had—as the shrewd pontiff hoped—soon turned Robert's acquisitive eye toward the Saracen-held island. In 1057, 26-year-old Roger—youngest and last of the Hauteville brothers to seek his fortune in the south—had joined Robert Guiscard. Roger's talents, rivaling those of Robert, soon became manifest. A 28-year partnership ensued that saw the brothers found a brilliant kingdom and dominate a glittering age. As their first joint venture, they attacked Sicily.

In May, 1061, the Normans assembled an array of men and ships on the Calabrian coast across from the key city of Messina. Under cover of night, 13 ships carried Roger and 270 horsemen to an obscure beach south of the sleeping city. Military historian D. P. Waley believes that this complex and unprecedented amphibious operation involving cavalry set the pattern for William the Conqueror's crossing of the English Channel five years later.

Roger and his knights took Messina handily, and the invasion of Sicily commenced under the most favorable auspices. But the auguries were false; not until 10 years later did the Normans capture Palermo, and yet another 20 years of local warfare would ensue before all of Sicily passed under Christian control. From the beginning of their conquest, however, the two Hautevilles imposed a policy of religious and racial tolerance unique in 11th-century Europe. Their charters guaranteed that "Latins, Greeks, Jews, and Saracens shall be judged each according to their own law." Skilled Moslem and Greek bureaucrats were retained in office, and the Hautevilles recruited Saracen brigades into their army.

While Roger doggedly rooted out pockets of Moslem resistance on the island, Robert sought ever broader horizons. In 1081 he perceived an opportunity to seize the most enticing of prizes—the throne of Byzantium. The empire, wracked by civil war, lay in disarray. Amassing a huge fleet and a mammoth army, Robert struck across the Adriatic. He established a beachhead on the Greek coast and captured the island of Corfu from its Byzantine garrison. But at Durazzo—now Durrës in Albania—he encountered a Greek army commanded by a new and strong emperor, Alexius I Comnenus, father of the Princess Anna. In the Byzantine vanguard marched the Varangians, now composed largely of Anglo-Saxon refugees from England, all eager to avenge the defeat of Hastings on the Norman knights.

As ever, the Varangians fought with breathtaking valor. Stationed on the left of the Byzantine line, they hurled themselves against the Norman cavalry—an unprecedented act in an age when the proper role of infantrymen was to be cut down at the pleasure of their mounted betters. With their monstrous battle-axes the Varangians slashed both knights and horses. Undone as much by the insolence of the attack as by its violence, the Norman flank collapsed.

But the rematch between Normans and Anglo-Saxons merely confirmed the outcome of the Battle of Hastings. Apulian crossbowmen zeroed in on the pursuing Varangians, now far in advance of the Byzantine line, and systematically slaughtered them. With the flower of his army destroyed, Alexius fled. The highway to Constantinople and an imperial crown yawned wide before Robert Guiscard. The duke and his men pushed down it, pausing to take Macedonia and part of Thessaly.

At this critical moment, the drearily predictable mutinies of his barons

Half-Italian, half-Norman, Count Roger II learns arithmetic from an Arab tutor. Assuming power in A.D. 1111 at age 16, the count nurtured in Sicily a culture rich in the elegances of East and West.

called Robert back to Italy. Mixing savagery with generosity, as was his wont, he soon restored order among his vassals; but the swirling chaos of Italian politics found his ally, Pope Gregory VII, under siege in Rome's Castel Sant' Angelo. The German troops of the Holy Roman Emperor, Henry IV, had invested the city, with the aim of enthroning a puppet anti-pope. In a misguided act that Robert Guiscard would cause them bitterly to regret, the citizenry of Rome had declared against Gregory. Thus, in the spring of 1084, the Duke of Apulia advanced up the peninsula with an overpowering force. Apprised of this development, Henry IV departed Rome in haste with most of his troops. It must have been a heady moment for Guiscard: Within four years, the former brigand had routed both the Emperor of the East and the Emperor of the West.

His columns smashed into the Eternal City despite desperate resistance, freed the Pope, and escorted him to the Lateran Palace. Then, led by the Saracens from Sicily, they pillaged and burned without pity. For Rome the devastation exceeded anything seen in more than 600 years.

His Italian fences mended effectively, if violently, Robert hurried back to Greece. The campaign had bogged down hopelessly and, though Guiscard's return inspired a few more victories, the winter of 1085 brought the Byzantines a new and decisive ally. A devastating disease—probably typhoid—ravaged the Normans, and in July it struck down the seemingly indestructible duke himself at the age of 68.

They buried him not in the splendid cathedral he had built in Salerno, but in the Abbey Church of the Most Holy Trinity in Venosa beside his brothers, William, Drogo, and Humphrey. His epitaph, wondrously simple and wondrously true, began: *Hic terror mundi Guiscardus* ... "Here lies the Guiscard, terror of the world."

From Capua south as you journey in Italy, you pass the ruins of Norman castles and abbeys. But the barons left few other traces in the land. I remember a Sunday in the decaying town of Mileto in Calabria, once the capital of Roger I. An Italian gentleman had guided me to the only extant relics of Mileto's Great Age: a well, a wall, and a few fallen columns from a Benedictine monastery built by the Normans 900 years ago. Bees buzzed in the stillness, and the scent of wild fennel perfumed the air. As we passed many small ruins, he muttered, "*Tutti abbandonati!*" And that, despite the brave and brilliant men who conquered Apulia and Calabria, sums up the fate of Norman Italy: "All abandoned!"

The death of Robert Guiscard left Roger, who soon became known as the Great Count, with a free hand in Sicily. As described by a chronicler, Geoffrey Maleterra, Roger was "wise in counsel, far-sighted in the ordering of affairs." And so he proved to be in welding together the disparate human elements of Sicily. Roger established four official languages: Arabic, Greek, Latin, and Norman French. The Saracen brigades constituted the chief striking force of his army; Moslems also furnished the backbone of the Sicilian bureaucracy. He endowed Greek Orthodox monasteries and appointed Latin bishops. When crusading fever swept Europe in 1096 and no less than six Hautevilles took the cross, Roger—in deference to his Moslem subjects—did not join them. Guiscard's son Bohemund, however, did leave Italy and sail eastward. A blond giant in the image of his father, he became the bane of both Christian and infidel in the Holy Land, seized the Biblical city of Antioch, and ended his days as its anointed prince.

The Great Count's failure to proselyte the Moslems of Sicily earned some criticism. The monk Eadmer, traveling with St. Anselm, recorded a curious episode during one of Roger's Italian campaigns. His Saracens were encamped near the lodgings of Anselm and sought him out. Wrote Eadmer: "They gratefully accepted offerings of food from Anselm and returned to their own people making known the wonderful kindness which they had experienced at his hands. As a result he was from this time held in such veneration among them, that when we passed through their camp ... a huge crowd of them, raising their hands to heaven, would call down blessings on his head. ... Many of them, even as we discovered, would willingly have submitted themselves to his instructions and would have allowed the yoke of the Christian faith to be placed by him upon their shoulders, if they had not feared ... the cruelty of their Count would have been let loose against them. For in truth he was unwilling to allow any of them to become Christian with impunity."

In 1101, the Great Count died and, after a short regency, his son Roger succeeded him as ruler of Sicily. The boy had come of age amid the orange trees and fragrant gardens of Palermo. Greek and Arabic tutors had instructed him in the graces and the sciences. When he attained manhood, he personified all the sophistication and cosmopolitanism of Sicily. He was also a consummate politician. In exchange for Norman military aid in times of need, Roger persuaded the Pope in 1130 to present him with a crown. "And so," wrote a witness to the ceremony in Palermo, "when the Duke was led in royal state to the Cathedral, and was there anointed with the holy oil and invested with the dignity of kingship, the splendour of his majesty and the magnificence of his apparel were beyond the power of words to express or imagination to conceive. . . ."

Although the island had known only poverty for more than a thousand years, riches became a fact of life in Norman Sicily. Pouring into the royal treasury were tolls to the value of ten percent of the cargo of every ship passing through the Strait of Messina — and the commerce was lively. Roger's income from the city of Palermo alone far exceeded that of his Norman counterpart, the King of England, from his entire realm. And Palermo? The great Arab geographer, al-Idrisi, who spent more than 20 years in Roger's court, called it "the greatest and finest metropolis in the world, and its beauties are infinite. . . . All around it there are plentiful channels of water and every kind of fruit. Its buildings dazzle the eye. . . ."

Roger's kingdom represented a small miracle of synthesis. A Greek, Georgios of Antioch, commanded his navy. A cool, high-living, and infinitely capable Englishman, Robert of Selby, served as his viceroy in the Italian peninsula. The coinage, as often as not, was dated according to the Arabic calendar; official documents sometimes bore dates based on the Greek system; Arabic inscriptions decked Christian churches, and often the churches themselves — several examples have survived in Palermo — strongly resembled mosques.

The terminology of public office reflected the same fusion. Judges were either *Justiciars* (Latin) or *Cadis* (Arabic); civil and military administrators might bear the Greek appellations of *Logothete* or *Strategos;* the king's chief minister rejoiced in the magnificent title of *Emir of Emirs.*

Roger's early training had left him with a passion for science and poetry, and he took pains to surround himself with men of letters — most of them, perforce, Arabs. He conversed with them at length in their own language. At Roger's commission, al-Idrisi devoted 15 years to assembling the most important compendium of geographical knowledge to emerge from the Middle Ages — one which, more than three centuries before Columbus, pointed out that the world was round. To this day in the lands of Islam, the book is known as *Kitāb Rujjār — The Book of Roger.*

In a startling anticipation of our own age, the king employed a diver, one Nicolas Papa, to explore the depths of the Strait of Messina and discover the secrets of the currents.

Roger — as did his successors William I and William II — kept a harem. Indeed, one Moslem visitor to Sicily reported of Roger "that the Christians of

F*ading light at day's end silhouettes the broken façade and two octagonal towers of the Notre-Dame Church at the ruins of the Abbey of Jumièges, beside the Seine. Vikings plundered the abbey three times in the ninth century, but penitent Normans restored it.*

the country accused him of being himself, also, in his heart of hearts, a Muslim."

Romuald, Archbishop of Salerno, described one of Roger's pleasure domes: "In order that none of the joys of the land or water should be lacking to him, he caused a great sanctuary for birds and beasts to be built at a place called Favara, which was full of caves and dells; its waters he stocked with every kind of fish from divers regions; nearby he built a beautiful palace."

But the king by no means devoted himself exclusively to leisure and study. In the 1140's his fleet undertook a campaign of conquest in North Africa that, when it ended, left him master of the littoral from Tripoli to Tunis. Sicilian squadrons also ravaged Greece, and even sailed up the Bosporus to menace Constantinople.

Roger died in 1154 of "exhaustion from his immense labours, and the onset of a premature senility through his addiction to the pleasures of the flesh. . . ." His son succeeded him, and then his grandson, but neither possessed the gift of statecraft. Surrounded by envious enemies, ruled by unworthy kings, Sicily slid toward the shadows. Before the 12th century ended, the Norman dynasty perished; the Moslems of Sicily fled to North Africa, the Greeks departed for Byzantium. Sicily, raised briefly from the ashes of history by the brilliance of the two Rogers, slipped back and has remained in many ways a bitter and burnt-out land ever since.

A few monuments to that lost glory still stand: Roger II's lovely cathedral beside the sea at Cefalù; the Cathedral of Monreale, a product of Arab architects and Greek craftsmen, its walls ablaze with more than 70,000 square feet of Byzantine mosaics; the exquisite Palatine Chapel—to enter it, wrote Guy de Maupassant, "is like walking into a jewel."

Several leading families of Sicily claim Norman ancestry. One day as I wandered through Palermo, I recalled a story told me by M. Lechanteur back in Caen. One of his colleagues, like himself an enthusiast of Norman history, had journeyed to Sicily. He had the address of a Sicilian authority, and duly knocked upon the door of a fine old house. An elderly lady of noble mien answered. To the man's confusion, it seemed that he had come to the wrong street.

"Where are you from?" the lady inquired in French.

"Normandy."

"*Entrez, vous êtes chez vous,*" she said, throwing wide the door. "Enter, you are at home."

The world may well weep for Sicily. Shaped by Guiscard and the two Rogers, far-farers from the sea-mists and apple orchards of Normandy, it glowed, for its brief century, with an ideal of tolerance and brotherhood and beauty—a brilliant, transitory preamble to the Renaissance. In the 800 years since its fall, we have not seen its like. So we mourn for all mankind when we mourn that sunshot kingdom of the sea, splendid even in its doom.

*C*aptured during the sack of her father's city, Popa, daughter of the Count of Bayeu

ands before Hrolf the Ganger in his camp. Hrolf married his beautiful prisoner.

Sealing a bargain, tradesmen in Isigny-sur-Mer, France (right), slap open palms as a sign of agreement. Farmers in Varde, Denmark (below), and York, England, close their dealings in the same way. Slapping the hand to indicate accord harks back to the Viking Age: Norse traders solemnly completed transactions with a handsala, *a vigorous striking together of palms.*

Benedictine monks gathered for community worship listen

to part of the liturgy (above) and later embrace for the

kiss of peace at the Abbey of St.-Wandrille, France.

Hooded brothers read as they walk past the chapel in the

abbey's park. In 858 the monks of St.-Wandrille fled

after repeated Viking raids; a century later the monastery

reopened and became a center of culture under Norman rule.

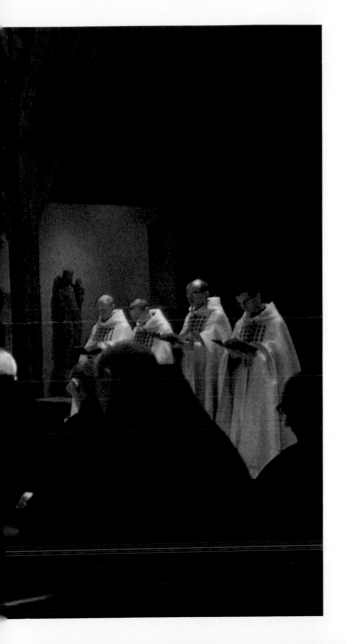

Ruins of Falaise Castle—birthplace of William the Conqueror—crown
a green hillside in Normandy. William, seventh Duke of Normandy
and a descendant of Hrolf the Ganger, sits a charging steed at
Falaise. Victorious in the Battle of Hastings in 1066, he captured the
English throne only 19 days after Hardraada failed in a similar quest.

END OF "A WIND AGE,

icily represented a radiant epilogue to the saga of Viking adventure. The last Norman kings of the South wore silken robes, passed languid days in their harems, and spoke Arabic or Greek as a matter of choice; they had made an epic voyage of the spirit from their ancestral fjords and islands. Yet, though their Viking blood had thinned en route, to the end they possessed the Viking thrust, the Viking flair, the Viking love of glory.

But it was only an afterglow. A century before Roger II claimed his crown in Palermo Cathedral, the world of the Northmen had begun to disintegrate. The attempted settlement of Vinland marked the zenith of Norse expansion; the failure in North America coincided with the onset of decline. The settlements in Greenland fell prey to hardship and misfortune. Further, with the end of the Viking Age came a decay of Norse seamanship. By the 14th century few captains were willing or able to cross the Atlantic, and first the Greenlanders, then the Icelanders were abandoned to their own resources. For Greenland, as we have seen, the isolation proved fatal. Sometime around 1500 the last remnant of the Norse population — its very existence forgotten by Europe — died or departed. No one knows which; no one knows why.

Alone among the far-flung western colonies, Iceland survived. And, because of its long solitude, it survived largely as an avatar of the 11th century. Among Scandinavians, only the Faeroese and the Icelanders still speak variants of Old Norse, the language of the Vikings. Locked in its medieval loneliness, Iceland immortalized the Viking era — "a wind age, a wolf age" — in the sagas, one of the world's great literary forms.

Most of the sagas — the Old Norse word means "telling" — date from the 13th century, when Iceland experienced a golden age of literature. The tradition, incidentally, continues: Modern Iceland publishes more books per capita than any other nation in the world. In 1955 the Icelandic novelist Halldor Laxness received the Nobel Prize for Literature.

The 13th-century sagamen synthesized their accounts of the heroes and families of Viking times from three sources: oral tradition, or folk tales; poems and verses; documents dealing with particular men or events. The greatest of them, Snorri Sturluson, explained in a preface how he had assembled the material for his saga history of the Scandinavian kings, *Heimskringla (The Orb of the World)*. His book contained "old stories about the rulers who have had kingdoms in Scandinavia and who spoke the Danish tongue, according to how I have heard learned men tell them; also, some of their family trees, as I myself have been taught them. Some of this is to be found in the genealogies in which kings and other men of distinguished birth have traced their descent; but some of it is written according to old poems or historical lays, which people have used to entertain themselves with. And although we do not know the truth of them, we do, however, know of examples when old and learned men have reckoned them to be true."

My first visit to Iceland introduced me rather rudely to a geological reality.

A WOLF AGE"

MILTON A. FORD AND VICTOR R. BOSWELL, JR., N.G.S. STAFF, WITH SPECIAL AUTHORIZATION OF THE CITY OF BAYEUX

Bayeux Tapestry depicts the Norman invasion of 1066 (top), the Battle of Hastings (center), the death of King Harold Godwinson (bottom, far right).

With his staff King Olaf Tryggvason of Norway destroys the image of Thor, as pagan followers of Olaf's enemy Ironbeard watch in horror. Soon subdued by the king's army, they embraced the Christianity brought by Olaf from England in 995.

I was in an eight-story building, one of the newest in Reykjavik, when suddenly the entire structure shuddered violently. A distant explosion, I thought, or perhaps a murderously low jet. But the spasm continued through a long and ugly 20 seconds. With all the composure of ignorance, I watched people dashing for the exits. Not until the final, convulsive shudder did I realize that I was experiencing my first earthquake. It proved to be the most violent shock recorded in earthquake-prone Reykjavik in several decades.

The tremor forcibly reminded me that Iceland is still in its geological youth, still in effect suffering growing pains. Geysers (the word derives from Old Norse) spew from the surface of the inner highlands. Glaciers, relics of the still-waning Ice Age, creep past smoldering volcanoes. And in 1963 the ocean south of Iceland suddenly spurted ash-laden clouds and the island of Surtsey rose full blown above the surface, a geologic Aphrodite of black lava.

In the depths of the Icelandic winter, dawn doesn't break until almost noon. It was still pitch dark at 10 a.m. on a December day when I was received in his office by Dr. Kristján Eldjárn, famous historian and President of Iceland.

I asked Dr. Eldjárn's opinion of the historicity of Iceland's most revered product, the sagas.

"There is general agreement," he said, "that the sagas mix fiction with historical elements. The difficulty lies in determining which is which.

"Icelandic culture stems to a very large degree from the Viking Age. Our language is the most important and most obvious example. Our natural

resources haven't improved; we still farm and fish for a living. Nor has the structure of our community changed in any essential way. When in the year 1000 the Althing adopted Christianity as the official religion, it was the pagan Thorgeir of Ljosavatn who announced that all should be baptized. And all were. There was no bloodshed, no persecution. Icelanders are still just as devoted to democratic procedures."

The twilight of the gods foreshadowed the twilight of the Vikings. Christianity's ultimate triumph, when it came, shattered ethical patterns and codes of conduct throughout Scandinavia. The process of conversion was slow, fitful, and often suffered serious reverses; but once the kings and jarls accepted baptism — as they did in increasing numbers at the beginning of the 11th century — the old gods lost Valhalla.

In 831, barely 40 years after the Vikings burst upon the western world, the Christian Church mounted a spiritual counterattack. The emperor of the Franks, Louis the Pious, in an action promptly confirmed by the papacy, named Hamburg "as the metropolitan see for all the barbarous nations of the Danes, the Swedes, and likewise the Slavs and the other peoples living round about."

The bishops of Hamburg thereafter dispatched waves of missionaries into the North. Though the harvest of souls was slight, many an evangelist won a martyr's crown. Adam of Bremen recorded the fate of one Wolfred, an Englishman, who "entered Sweden and with great courage preached the Word of God. . . . he proceeded to anathematize a popular idol named Thor which stood in the

Thing of the pagans, and at the same time he seized a battle ax and broke the image to pieces. And forthwith he was pierced with a thousand wounds for such daring. . . ."

But there were exceptions. Poppo, "a holy and wise man" according to Adam—and, from the evidence, a gifted showman—scored a spectacular success in Denmark. "Since it is the way of barbarians to seek after a sign, he straightway and without hesitation held a red-hot iron in his hand and seemed to be unharmed. Although it would appear that every delusion of error should by this act easily have been removed from the minds of the pagans, the saint of God is said once again to have manifested another miracle—if you will, a greater one—in order to clear away that people's paganism. For he clad himself in a waxed tunic and, standing in the midst of the people, directed that it be set on fire in the name of the Lord. Then, with his eyes and hands lifted up to heaven, he so patiently bore the spreading flames that, after his garment was entirely consumed and reduced to ashes, his cheerful and pleasant countenance gave proof of his having not even felt or suffered from the smoke of the fire. Because of this unusual miracle many thousands then believed through him and to this very day Poppo's name is extolled by the peoples and in the churches of the Danes."

Despite the substantial missionary effort, most Vikings probably came to Christianity through their exposure to it in the lands they visited to the south. Here and there a Norseman embraced Christianity as early as the first quarter of the tenth century, and toward its end very many had been "prime-signed." The Christian ceremony of *prima signatio* was the first step on the road toward baptism. For pagans it apparently represented a kind of *laissez passer* to Christian society. *Egil's Saga* explains that prime-signing was common among Norse traders and "those who went on war-pay along with Christian men"; Northmen who had been prime-signed "held full communion with Christians and heathens too, yet kept the faith which was most agreeable to them."

The evidence suggests that early Norse converts shared a rather unorthodox view of their new religion. Polytheists by tradition, they tended to accept Christ as a new and more powerful, but by no means an only, god. Thus Helgi the Lean of Iceland "believed in Christ, and yet made vows to Thor for sea-voyages and in tight corners, and for everything which struck him as of real importance." Nor did conversion work any profound cultural or moral miracles among the Scandinavians. Blood feuds continued unabated; so did the putting to death by exposure of unwanted infants; and so did polygamy among the ruling classes. Rather testily, Adam of Bremen found fault with the young Danish dioceses: "Bishops, for example, sold their blessing, the people would not pay tithes, and everybody far exceeded moderation in respect of eating and of women."

From the first days of conversion, the new Christians held their priests—who were generally foreigners—personally responsible as the representatives of Jesus for the vagaries of life and nature. In the 11th century, Pope Gregory VII complained that the Scandinavians would "transfer the blame to the priests for the intemperate . . . seasons, for pestilences of the air, and all ills of the flesh."

As more Northmen attained priestly status, the quality of the office degenerated. Priests clothed themselves in everyday garb and even carried weapons. Celibacy was not enforced. In the North, landowners built churches on their estates and retained ownership; they hired clergy to staff them much as they would hire other servants. Some of the Scandinavian priests were barely 16 years old, few could cope with Latin, and all were subject to the outlaw code if they ran away. The year 1200 brought the priests a modicum of dignity when the Gulathing Law proclaimed that "we [the yeomen] have abolished the practice of disciplining them with blows, because we give them our daughters and sisters in marriage or let our own sons be educated as clergymen."

Just as Rome succumbed to Christianity only when the emperors embraced it, so did the sea kings of Scandinavia blaze the way for their subjects. Many of the tenth-century kings—for example, Harald Greycloak of Denmark and Haakon the Good of Norway—became Christian but either failed to proselyte or reverted to the old gods. The first to remain constant was Harald Bluetooth of Denmark, who converted rather late in life. He raised a runestone at Jelling, once a pagan sanctuary, memorializing himself as "that Harald who won for himself all Denmark and Norway, and made the Danes Christian."

Next to embrace the new faith was Norway's energetic Olaf Tryggvason. After an early life during which he was captured by pirates, went viking in the Baltic, and won the love of various Rus and Slavic ladies, he apparently fought in England at the Battle of Maldon, and subsequently served as an ally of Svein Forkbeard. Sometime around 995 in England, Olaf paid his momentous visit to the baptismal font; thereafter he became a ruthless cutting edge for the Gospel. Images of the northern gods and sanctuaries alike fell before his righteous wrath, and he abided paganism nowhere—least of all among his skalds. All but one of them, Hallfred, bent to the royal will in the matter of religion. But Hallfred "did not vilify the gods." Hectored by the king, Hallfred composed a verse that rather touchingly illuminates the inability of this new Christian to hate his old gods:

> Odin, in your praise　Poets have always written
> Godsent verse; well should I　Remember this.
> Nor would I—for the Skaldmaster's　Gift meets mine—
> Now hate Frigg's mighty　Lord, though I serve Christ.

Religion troubled Hallfred throughout his life. At the end, with Valhalla gone, he could only fear hell, and in his last sickness he composed this verse:

> I would die now　Soon and sorrow-free
> If I knew my soul was safe—　Young I was sharp of tongue;
> I know I grieve for nothing—　Everyone must die—
> But I fear hell; let God　Decide where I wear out my time.

The mightiest royal champion of Christ in the North was Norway's Olaf Haraldsson, Olaf the Stout—later to become (Continued on page 183)

Mired in clay that had served as a preservative, the Oseberg burial
ship undergoes excavation. Archeologists found the ship in 1904 in
thousands of fragments. Painstakingly they marked and numbered each one,
treated it with creosote and linseed oil, and pressed it into its
original shape for reconstruction. At left, a Danish Senior Scout works
on the Imme Gram, a replica of the Ladby ship, at Haderslev; above,
a crew member holds a rigging detail copied from the Gokstad ship.

*S*couts at Augustenborg launch the Sebbe Als, *a copy of a small warship found at Skuldelev in Roskilde Fjord in 1962. Below, another lad examines oars handcarved for this ship but modeled on the Gokstad oars. Two scouts struggle to fasten a piece of the rigging in another replica,* Imme Drøpner.

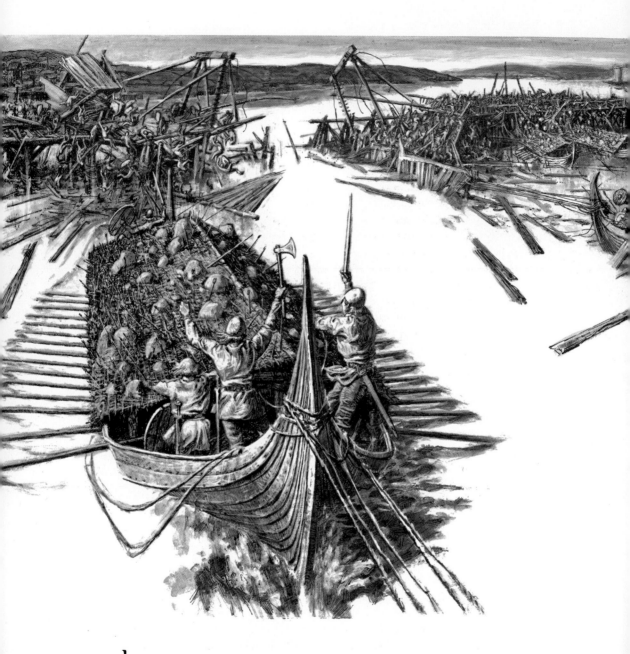

*L*ondon Bridge is falling down: Having roofed his ships for protection,

    Olaf Haraldsson tied hawsers to the bridge pilings and rowed hard

downstream, toppling the bridge into the Thames.

his country's patron saint—who also pursued a distinguished career as a Viking. Early in the 11th century, while still in his teens, he served in England under the command of Thorkell the Tall. According to *St. Olaf's Saga,* sometime around 1010 he led a fleet up the Thames and pulled down London Bridge:

"Olaf had large hurdles made of withies and soft wood, so cut as to make a wickerhouse, and thus covered his ships, so that the hurdles reached out over their sides; he had posts put beneath them so high that it was easy to fight beneath them, and the covering was proof against stones thrown down on it. When the host was ready they rowed up the river; as they came near the bridges they were shot at, and such large stones thrown down on them that neither their helmets nor shields could withstand them; and the ships themselves were greatly damaged, and many retreated. But Olaf and the Northmen with him rowed up under the bridges, and tied ropes round the supporting posts, and rowed their ships downstream as hard as they could. The posts were dragged along the bottom until they were loosened from under the bridges. As an armed host stood thickly on the bridges, and there was a great weight of stones and weapons upon them, and the posts beneath were broken, the bridges fell with many of the men into the river; the others fled into the city, or into Southwark."

A very old tradition holds that this incident inspired the nursery rhyme:

> *London Bridge is falling down,*
> *Falling down, falling down.* . . .

In 1013, after adventuring in France, Olaf received baptism at the hands of his Norman cousins in Rouen. The following year found the convert raiding the beleaguered Christian provinces of northern Spain. Inasmuch as these enclaves were battling desperately for survival against the encroachments of the powerful Moors, Olaf's conduct prompted the great Dutch historian of Moslem Spain, Dozy, to comment drily: "This was a saint of a singular type."

In 1016 Olaf ascended the throne of Norway and, for the brief two years of his reign, evangelized his countrymen with unflagging zeal. Above all, reports Adam of Bremen, Olaf "routed out the magicians from the land. Although all barbarism overflows with their number, the Norwegian land in particular was full of these monsters."

Ardent for converts, Olaf burned down the farms of all who resisted the divine word; nor did he shrink from blinding and maiming those of his subjects hardened in error.

Whatever the methods, they worked. When Harald Bluetooth's son, Svein Forkbeard, became King of Denmark about 985, he was a Christian monarch ruling a largely Christian land. And when Svein's son Knut forged England and most of Scandinavia into a North Sea Empire, Christians constituted the majority of his subjects.

Thus the dawn of the 11th century saw the cross of Christ supplanting the hammer of Thor throughout the developing kingdoms of the North. Only in remote Sweden, the ultimate bastion of European paganism, did Odin and his pantheon survive for yet a few more generations.

Christianity spelled the end of the way of life that had sired the Viking Age. Now eternal damnation, rather than Valhalla, awaited warriors slain while ravaging and murdering. Charity replaced ruthlessness in the catalogue of virtues, as mercy replaced rapine. Trading in slaves—now largely the delivering of co-religionists into infidel hands—grew ever more repugnant to the new Christians.

While the gentling precepts of the New Testament gradually debilitated the Vikings' warlike qualities, a military reverse in Ireland—the Battle of Clontarf in 1014—sent a shudder of foreboding throughout the North. The battle came as the climax of a 50-year campaign by the Irish prince Brian Boru to control the foreigners and, in the process, to secure the High Kingship. Brian found the road to power paved with suffering and reverses. Recounts a 12th-century Irish chronicle: "Great . . . were the hardship and the ruin, the bad food and bad bedding which they inflicted on him in the wild huts of the desert, on the hard, knotty, wet roots of his own native country. . . ."

But Brian persevered in his attacks upon the heathen; soon victory succeeded victory. In 968, with his brother Mathgamhain, he defeated the Norse of Limerick and sacked their rich commercial port. A writer of the time tabulated the booty won by the Irish: "They carried off their jewels and their best property, and their saddles beautiful and foreign; their gold and their silver; their beautifully woven cloth of all colours and of all kinds; their satins and silken cloth, pleasing and variegated, both scarlet and green, and all sorts of cloth in like manner. They carried away their soft, youthful, bright, matchless girls; their blooming silk-clad young women; and their active, large, and well-formed boys. The fort and the good town they reduced to a cloud of smoke and to red fire afterwards. The whole of the captives were collected on the hills of Saingel. Every one of them that was fit for war was killed, and every one that was fit for a slave was enslaved."

This "fierce, bloody, crimsoned, violent, rough, unsparing, implacable battle" was only one of 25 fought by Brian in pursuit of his goal. In the year 1000, his strength waxing, he moved against Sigtrygg Silkbeard, the Norse king of Dublin. The Irish prevailed and their forces sacked the city. Sigtrygg managed to weather the storm and, in its wake, even maintained a shaky rule in Dublin. But the victorious Brian became High King in 1002, and his reign brought order and serenity to Ireland for the first time in 200 years. "After Erinn was reduced to a state of peace," marveled a chronicler, "a lone woman came from Torach, in the north of Erinn, to Cliodhna, in the south of Erinn, carrying a ring of gold . . . and she was neither robbed nor insulted. . . ."

Throughout the North, men soon realized that Brian's victories were sowing the seeds of Norse doom. So Vikings from all the Norse realms, from Iceland to Normandy, thronged to Ireland at Sigtrygg's urging to challenge the High King's sovereignty in a decisive battle at Clontarf. The human mosaic of opposing forces arrayed there lacked consistency, however: Many an Irish Viking, deeply involved in the politics of Erin, fought with Brian; and many a dissident Gael joined the invading Northmen.

The Annals of Loch Cé listed the opposing armies at Clontarf. Brian—now at least 80 years old—made "a great hosting" of the men of Munster, Meath, and the south of Connaught. Against him stood the Irish of Leinster and the "choicest of brave men" from Viking England, Denmark, and Norway, as well as troops from Orkney, the Hebrides, Man, and Scotland. The Jarl of York led a contingent, as did Uither Dubh from Cornwall, Grisine of the Flemings, and Gresham of the Normans.

The hosts clashed on Good Friday, 1014, in a "furious, barbarous, smashing onset." The Jarl of Orkney, wreaking great havoc among the Irish, died when one of Brian's commanders "cut his neck and felled that brave hero with two tremendous, well-aimed blows." Brian Boru, grown old and infirm in his quest of power, had pitched his tent in a wood and, while the battle raged, prayed quietly. But Brodir of the Isle of Man, roaming behind the Irish lines, discovered the High King and "dealt Brian a stroke which cleft his head utterly." But to Brodir's profound misfortune, the vengeful Irish quickly took him alive. The saga accounts describe gruesome torturing of the prisoner; Irish scholars insist torture was not the Celtic way. In any event, Brodir did not survive the day.

Before the sun set, 4,000 of the Irish found death, and 7,000 of the Norse. Sigtrygg Silkbeard, who had started it all, won instant Irish pardon by barring the gates of Dublin to the pitiful Norse survivors.

The Viking rout at Clontarf generated a pall of despair that spread throughout the North. A famous poem in *Njál's Saga* crystallized the sense of doom, the stunning realization that the long series of Norse victories had ended forever. An Icelander named Dorrud supposedly experienced a horrible vision on the Good Friday of the battle. Women at the ghastly loom of history chanted:

> *Lands will be ruled   By new peoples*
> *Who once inhabited   Outlying headlands.*
> *We pronounce a great king   Destined to die;*
> *Now an earl   Is felled by spears.*
> *The men of Ireland   Will suffer a grief*
> *That will never grow old   In the minds of men.*
> *The web is now woven   And the battlefield reddened;*
> *The news of disaster   Will spread through lands.*

While Clontarf spelled doom in Ireland, it was only a melancholy splinter in the chaos of fragmentation that convulsed the 11th-century northern world. War raged almost constantly among the three Scandinavian states. Iceland declared independence. The Normandy Vikings, thoroughly Gallicized, rebuffed the raids of their former brethren. With the collapse of Knut's North Sea Empire, Anglo-Saxon monarchs reascended the English throne.

Adding to Norse misfortune, professional armies had become the rule rather than the exception throughout western Europe. No longer could an adventuring fleet expect to find unprotected coasts and towns. So the Viking Age slowly faded in a diminuendo of dissension, civil war, and defeat.

Through these darkling decades flashed a final human meteor—the most ferocious, cultured, and vivid of the sea kings: Harald Sigurdsson, called Hardraada, or Hard Ruler, who reigned over Norway from 1047 to 1066.

As a boy of 15, Harald had been blooded in battle at the side of his half-brother, Olaf the Stout. Partly because of King Olaf's harsh evangelizing, partly because the jarls of Norway resisted centralized control of the country, Olaf had been deposed after a short and turbulent reign. He sought refuge with his kinsman Yaroslav the Wise and, after a sojourn in Russia, determined to regain his throne. With some 3,600 men, including Harald, he smashed across the Swedish border in 1030 but was overwhelmingly defeated by the Norwegians who, quite literally, wanted no more of their erstwhile ruler. Olaf perished —to receive at once the name Olaf the Saint. Harald, though severely wounded, managed to escape the rout of his half-brother's followers and to slip away to Russia, where he too was given sanctuary in the glittering court of Yaroslav. There the Norwegian youth also found love, in the person of Yaroslav's daughter, Yelisaveta.

On the heights of Kiev the golden domes of the Cathedral of St. Sophia glitter against the blue sky. Now a museum of architecture and history, the old church resounds to the footsteps of an endless stream of tourists both foreign and domestic, inspecting this sublime monument of the ancient Rus. Inside, I sought out a famous mural dating from the time of Harald. In colors muted by a thousand years, three daughters of Yaroslav gaze across the centuries. One of them is Anna, who became Queen of France and, to the bedazzlement of her court, could both read and write; the other two are Anastasia, future Queen of Hungary, and Yelisaveta, who would reign in Norway. Four of Yaroslav's sons also married royalty. A Ukrainian friend remarked, "No wonder our historians call Yaroslav the father-in-law of Europe."

All of the princesses possess a stately and formal beauty. But I found myself staring at Yelisaveta with her wide, haunted eyes, her mouth touched by tragedy, her hand extended in supplication—she who left the Byzantine elegance of her father's court to live out her life amid the crude farmsteads, blood feuds, and drunken, gluttonous revels of the North.

For three years Harald Sigurdsson fought valorously in the Viking cohort of Yaroslav's *druzhina*, or army. Although he sought Yelisaveta's hand, it was in vain; presumably the father-in-law of Europe did not fancy a throneless son-in-law. So, to seek his fortune, Harald followed the example of generations of Vikings; he sailed down the Dnieper to fabled Miklagård.

In Byzantium Harald joined the Varangian Guard, and soon became its commander. The year 1038 took him and his men to Sicily, where briefly the Varangians united forces with their distant kinsmen of Normandy under the command of the Greek general Georgios Maniakes. A Byzantine author chronicled Harald's career in the imperial service:

"The emperor received him as was seemly and proper, and dispatched him together with his company to Sicily . . . and he went there and achieved mightily. And when Sicily had been conquered he returned with his troops to the

Monks of Ely sing for Knut, able King of England and Denmark, as he sails past their monastery walls. During his prosperous reign from 1016 to 1035, the church found a strong champion.

emperor, who appointed him *manglavites* [belt-wearer]. . . . In Bulgaria . . . Araltes [Harald] and his company went campaigning with the emperor and achieved mightily . . . as befitted a man of his birth and bravery. . . . The emperor appointed Araltes *spatharokandates* [a post of honor in the imperial court] as a reward for his services."

For ten years Harald wielded sword and battle-ax for the empire, campaigning from the Greek islands to Asia Minor, from the Caucasus Mountains to Palestine. A fearsome figure, he towered almost seven feet in height. His saga reports him as fair of hair and beard, but "one of his eyebrows was slightly higher than the other." He accumulated incredible booty—a good part of it illegally, according to the same saga—and sent it back to Kiev.

But neither wealth nor honors could banish the Kievan princess from his mind. While in Byzantium he wrote a poem to his Gold Ring Gerd in Gard—a kenning for Yelisaveta. One stanza strikes a note of puzzled poignance:

> *I can brew Odin's draught [i.e., write verse]*
> *I am nimble on horseback,*
> *Have at times taken to swimming,*
> *I know tables, runes, book-reading,*
> *Harping, shooting, rowing,*
> *Carpentry, snow-skating, and poetry,*
> *Yet Gold Ring Gerd in Gard*
> *Ignores my suit.*

Harald's service in Byzantium was not free of adversity. William of

Malmesbury reports that when, at the emperor's command, Harald was "exposed to a lion, for having debauched a woman of quality, he strangled the huge beast by the bare vigour of his arms." And the endemic rapacity of the Norse also brought him to grief. Snorri Sturluson recounts that, because Harald misappropriated public money—either taxes he embezzled or loot he illegally withheld from the crown—he was thrown into jail.

In 1044, however, Harald regained his freedom and sailed back to Kiev. Yaroslav, who had banked Harald's booty and therefore knew firsthand of his resources, welcomed him and joyfully bestowed his daughter's hand upon this prince so full of promise. Harald returned to his native Norway with both Yelisaveta and "so much wealth, that in the Northern Countries nobody had ever seen anything like it in the possession of a single man." The combined thrust of Harald's personality and his gold brought him the crown in 1047.

His 19-year reign fully justified the cognomen *Hardraada*. In Byzantium Harald had seen autocracy in action and had found it much to his taste. To the unruly jarls of Norway he showed no mercy, and more than one of them he caused to "kiss the thin-lipped axe." In the words of the royal skald Thjodolf:

> *All the people humbly*
> *Bow before this warrior.*

On his magnificent longship *Dragon*, Harald bore his banner *Land-Waster* throughout Scandinavia, harrying, looting, destroying. In a climax of self-defeating Viking rage, he even burned the vital trading mart of Hedeby.

The king built churches and, as an echo of his years in the East, apparently introduced Orthodox missionaries into Norway and Iceland. But his ruthlessness never abated, and as a result the stories of his cruelty grew with retelling and the bias of the writer. Adam of Bremen—who called Harald "the Thunderbolt of the North"—wrote with more bitterness than accuracy that the Norwegian king "surpassed all the madness of tyrants in his savage wildness. Many churches were destroyed by that man; many Christians were tortured to death by him. . . . he was odious to all on account of his greed and cruelty. He also gave himself up to magic arts. . . ."

Amid the carnage, Harald seems to have made at least one voyage of exploration. "After he had explored the expanse of the Northern Ocean in his ships, there lay before their eyes at length the darksome bounds of a failing world, and by retracing his steps he barely escaped in safety the vast pit of the abyss."

Then, in 1066, Harald's gaze turned to the greatest prize a Viking heart could covet: England. The death of Edward the Confessor, as we have seen, left Earl Harold Godwinson in command of the kingdom. William the Bastard contested Harold's claim to the throne; so did Harald of Norway. As the clouds of conflict gathered, Harold Godwinson—whose courage was exceeded only by his bad luck—audaciously accepted crown, orb, and scepter in Westminster. He then prepared to defend his realm.

Harald Hardraada struck first. Reinforced by Earl Tostig, the English

Harold's own brother who himself lusted for the crown, and a complement of greedy Vikings from the Orkneys, the Norwegian king led 300 ships down the coast of Northumbria. Hardraada's host swarmed ashore at Riccall, handily defeated the English near York, and entered the city unopposed.

Then, unaccountably and completely, victory-luck ran out on the warrior who had sated the wolves from the Caucasus to the Apennines. After returning to his ships for several days, he split his army; leaving part of it with the fleet, he led the rest toward York to discuss terms with its chief citizens. Apparently the expedition had a kind of picnic air. "The weather was very hot and sunny," relates one chronicle, "and they left their mailshirts behind and went ashore with shields and helmets and spears and wore their swords and many had bows and arrows. They were very happy, with no thought of any attack, and when they were getting near the town they saw a great cloud of dust and under it bright shields and shining mail." It was the army of Harold Godwinson, and the English took the Norwegians by complete surprise. Cut off from the fleet and reinforcements, lacking even his coat of mail, the Norwegian king was forced to give battle on the pleasant morning of September 25.

Although much repaired and rebuilt, Stamford Bridge still arches across the Derwent about eight miles from York. Now, however, it bears the inevitable stigmata of the 20th century—a traffic light at either end. Under a lowering December sky, I walked out on the bridge to gaze across the meadows where the two kings had cast their deadly dice nine centuries before. Plows and shovels still occasionally turn up an arrowhead or a corroded sword blade, but no spell of battle lingers over this tranquil countryside.

I tried to envision that long-ago clash as memorialized by chroniclers and sagamen. The English, many of them mounted, had advanced from the west. As the Norse rallied around the banner *Land-Waster*, a troop of English horsemen galloped forward to parley with Harald and Tostig. The smallest hailed Tostig and offered him rule over half the kingdom if he would abandon the battle.

And what, asked Tostig, would the king confer upon Harald Sigurdsson?

"Seven feet of English ground—or as much more as he is taller than other men," came the reply.

"Make ready for battle," cried Tostig defiantly.

As the Englishmen clattered away, Harald asked, "Who was that man who spoke so well?"

"King Harold Godwinson."

"What a little man that was," Harald said thoughtfully, "but he stood proudly in his stirrups."

Then the poet-king—surely with fair Yelisaveta in mind—composed a verse for the occasion:

> *She told me once to carry*
> *My head always high in battle*
> *Where swords seek to shatter*
> *The skulls of doomed warriors.*

Recklessly the English smashed into the Norse shields. Spears reddened as the Valkyries sang; wound-dew drenched the grass; ravens swooped low for the banquet. The Norse shield-wall broke. The English tide engulfed *Land-Waster*. Then the Thunderbolt of the North "rushed forward ahead of his troops, fighting two-handed"—until an English arrow pierced his throat.

One tradition tells that Harald died in the arms of his skald Thjodolf, saying, "I will accept that piece of the kingdom that was offered me this morning."

"The remaining Norwegians," declares the Anglo-Saxon Chronicle, "were put to flight, while the English fiercely assailed their rear until some of them reached their ships; some were drowned, others burnt to death. . . ."

Without delay, Harold of England wheeled his forces southward to face the Norman threat. Ironically, he who had conquered the mightiest warrior of the Viking era would himself, in a matter of days, lose his kingdom and his life to William.

Meanwhile, Harald Hardraada's giant body lay still in the wake of battle. What final memory had fixed his glazing mind's eye? Was it the sight of the Dnieper cleaving the green heights of Kiev like molten jade . . . brocaded princesses gliding through the palaces of Byzantium . . . the lemon trees of Sicily and the April splash of Saracen fountains . . . *Dragon* plunging wild and free through the Atlantic?

This king had known the Viking world in all the wide, waning glory of its sunset. And when Harald Sigurdsson—Hard Ruler, Spatharokandates, Jerusalem-Farer, Poet—died at Stamford Bridge, the Viking Age sank finally below the horizon of history.

I stood on the bridge as dusk fell, bringing with it a light drizzle. No man or car had come this way, yet the imperious traffic lights continued to flash their signals into the unheeding mist. As I turned away, the light before me gleamed amber; the reflection glittered across the wet pavement like a slash of gold. The light switched to red; the gold became blood. Yellow and red, gold and blood—a fitting blazon for the era that had perished here.

Descending from the bridge, alone in all that lonely landscape, I recalled a verse of the olden time:

> *No man lives till eve*
> *Whom the fates doom at dawning.*

*U*ndaunted by rain, spectators crowd the hillside at the annual pageant honoring Norway's patron saint, Olaf Haraldsson. Battling to regain his kingdom, Olaf fell at Stiklarstadir in 1030. At right, in a scene of the play, the king miraculously heals a young woman.

SIGNY A. SPIEGEL (RIGHT

Symbol of the end of the Viking Age, a lone Norwegian warrior defies the English a

Stamford Bridge. But the Northmen lost the battle and withdrew at last from Britain.

Heirs of the Vikings in France and England claim Norse ancestry dating
from the late ninth century. François, Duc d'Harcourt (below), standing
before the ancestral castle in Normandy, and his distant English cousin
Viscount Harcourt, at his Oxfordshire estate, share forebears who
fought with Hrolf the Ganger when he invaded Normandy. Fisherman
Jean Anquetil of Auderville, France (opposite, left), descends from
Norse colonists of Neustria who came from Denmark in a longship.
Suffolk farmer George Thirkettle, whose name may have meant "kettle of
Thor," lives in the former Danelaw as his family has for centuries.

Christendom absorbs the pagan Viking world: On the altar of Urnes stave church, candles flame in a dragon ship. The church portal (opposite) displays refined late-Viking animal motifs. An 11th-century stone cross on the island of Kvitsøy, off the west coast of Norway, still guides seafarers.

The World the Vikings Knew

The Challenge
of the Sea-Roads

By JØRGEN JENSEN, Chief Navigator
Scandinavian Airlines System

ON THE DARK SEAS of the Dark Ages, men sailed timidly from headland to headland trying to keep in sight of shore. Yet before the Viking period had passed, enterprising Northmen had thrust westward to the Shetland and Faeroe Islands, then on to Iceland and Greenland, and—beyond the dreaming of the geographers of their time—to the east coast of North America.

We know that their ships improved greatly over those years; so did their skill in navigation. As the era advanced, as contacts with other countries increased, and as individuals of extraordinary talent emerged among them, the Vikings increased in knowledge of sea, earth, and sky. What did they learn? What navigational devices may they have discovered and brought into use?

First of all, the sailors of those days had to know seas and seamanship with an intimacy that seems almost incredible to us now. They were acute observers of sun and stars, currents and winds, sea creatures and land shapes—everything that could give them clues to direction, weather, and landfall; for their lives and livelihoods depended on clear perception and retentive memory.

As evidence of their distant voyaging, here are sailing directions given in the *Landnámabók (Book of the Landtakings)* of Iceland, first compiled before the middle of the 12th century: "According to learned men, it is seven days' sail from Stad in Norway to Horn in the east of Iceland; and from Snaefellsness [on the west coast of Iceland] it is four days' sail to Cape Farewell in Greenland. From Hernar in Norway to sail a direct course west

Network of the Vikings' routes emphasizes their epic achievement. For more than 250 years horizons fell before the northern adventurers: across western Europe, Russia, and the Near East, and—as they perfected their navigational skills—across uncharted seas to the New World.

Reykjavík

Faeroe
Islands

Shetland
Islands

Orkney
Islands

North Sea

Lindisfarne

Isle of Man

Dublin

York

DANELAW

London

Winchester

Bayeux

Rouen

Paris

Tours

Île de Noirmoutier

Lyon

Gijón

Toulouse

Pamplona

Madrid

Lisbon

Seville

Córdoba

Algeciras

Nekor

Balearic
Islands

Luna

Pisa

Rome

Messina

Palermo

Syracuse

Crete

Benghazi

Tripoli

Alexandria

Murmansk

Archangel

Lake
Ladoga

Stiklarstadir

Trondheim

Helsinki

Novgorod

Moscow

Hjørund Fjord

Uppsala

Stockholm

Oslo

Gokstad

Oseberg

Birka

Gotland

Smolensk

JUTLAND

Copenhagen

Roskilde

Ladby

Chernigov

Kiev

Vitichev

Berlin

Dorestad

Prague

Mainz

Vienna

Budapest

Bucharest

Stamford
Bridge

Black Sea

Istanbul
(Constantinople)

Baghdad

Beirut

Jerusalem

Caspian Sea

Baku

Gorgan

RICHARD SCHLECHT

to Hvarf [near Cape Farewell] in Greenland, you pass far enough north of the Shetlands that you sight land in clear weather only, then so much south of the Faeroes that only the upper half of the braes is visible above the sea, and then so much south of Iceland that you will see whales and birds."

Clearly the Vikings could maintain a course over the open ocean and follow fairly complicated directions. It is of no use to tell a sailor to "head west" unless he knows where west is. How would he have found his way?

Precisely when the magnetic compass was first used at sea is not known. The *Landnámabók* says that when Floki, the first Viking to consider settling in Iceland (and then to change his mind), sailed west just before 870, "in northern lands those who sailed the sea had no lodestone." In fact, one of the earliest mentions of the compass is by an Englishman, Alexander Neckam, who described in the 1180's a needle "placed upon a dart" and used by sailors when "they lose the advantage of the ... sun during cloudy weather."

By the Middle Ages the Norse had at least a pragmatic notion that the earth was round. A compendium of information written about 1250, the *Konungs Skuggsjá (The King's Mirror)*, contains the following dialogue between a young man learning the merchant's profession and his father, a canny, experienced man of the world.

The son: "You said that the sun ascends more rapidly to the north of us where there is hardly any summer. . . . But I have heard that in the southerly lands they do not suffer from the winter, and that the sun there is as warm during winter as it is here in summer. . . . If you can explain this so I can understand it, I will listen gladly. . . ."

The father: "I will begin with a simple illustration. . . . Light a candle and place it in a large room; it will then . . . throw its light all over the room. But if you take an apple and hang it so close to the candle that the apple gets warm, it will darken nearly half the room. . . . If you hang the apple close to the wall, it will not get warm and the candle lights all the room; where the apple hangs, the shadow on the wall will be scarcely half the size of the apple. From this we conclude that the earth-circle is round like a ball, and

not all places are equally close to the sun. The places where earth's curved surface is nearest the sun and that lie directly beneath its rays are uninhabitable. The countries, however, that are so placed that the sun's rays hit them obliquely are habitable, but some are warmer than others. . . ."

The sagas contain many examples— though unfortunately without much detail —of the northern sailor's habits of close observation. He had a good practical, if not very theoretical, understanding of ways to set and keep a course; much of his skill had to do with the rough determination of latitude.

About 1150 Abbot Nicolas of Tvaerå in Iceland went on a pilgrimage to the Holy Land. He wrote, "Out by Jordan if a man lies on flat ground, bends his knee, puts his hand on top and raises the thumb, then the polestar is just above the thumb and no higher." He clearly expected that the information would interest those at home. Leif Ericsson observed—and the record has been preserved for nearly a thousand years—that in Vinland "night and day were of more even length than in either Greenland or Iceland," and noted the length of the shortest day of the year from sunup to sundown.

There would be times, however, when the signs failed and even the skilled mariner was at a loss. The sagas had a word for this: *hafvilla*, getting lost at sea. This was especially likely when there was heavy fog and no wind, and all the clues of sky and sea were shrouded. Says the *Laxdaela Saga*: "They had poor weather that summer, with dense fogs and hardly any wind. . . . They drifted about all over the ocean, and most of the men on board lost all sense of direction."

Perhaps the most notable example of hafvilla occurred in 986 when the young captain Bjarni Herjulfsson, with directions from friends in Iceland, headed for a destination— Greenland—that he had never seen. He and his crew were out of sight of land when "the fair wind failed and northerly winds and fog set in. . . . After that they saw the sun again and were able to get their bearings . . . and after a day's sailing they sighted land." That land, which Bjarni apparently felt no urge to explore, was North America.

". . . they saw the sun again and were able to get their bearings. . . ." Is it possible that the Norse had developed a bearing dial?

In a ruin in Greenland's Eastern Settlement was found half of a wooden disk with a hole in the center and evenly spaced notches around the rim. The whole disk would have shown 32 notches (one would expect, in Viking times, such a division—first into the eight "eykts" of the old Norse horizon, then further subdivision of the eight sectors). The disk is dated about 1200.

Capt. Carl V. Sølver has reconstructed this implement as a bearing dial, though some critics disagree and no other example has been found. If it is such a dial, a shaft would be fitted in the center with an upright pin and a horizontal pointer. The dial could then be used to take bearings of the sun or of a known landmark: A sailor wishing to take his observation at noon waits till the altitude of the sun culminates. The time is then local noon. He holds the dial up, looks at the shadow of the pin and can tell where north is.

Perhaps the greatest scientific accomplishment of the late Viking Age was the work of an Icelander, Oddi Helgason. So fascinated by the observation of the heavens was he that he acquired the nickname Star-Oddi.

Around the middle of the 12th century he worked out a table giving the positions of the rising and setting sun from winter to summer solstice. Modern computation has proved the table correct to within three degrees. He also worked out the altitudes of the sun at noon for fortnightly intervals, using sun diameters and half diameters as the measuring scale. Star-Oddi was an astronomer, however, not a navigator, and scholars do not know how much practical use was made of his tables.

Perhaps the most interesting of the devices that might have been used in Viking navigation is the *solarstein*—the sunstone. An old saga story in the *Flateyjarbók* tells how King Olaf the Stout spent a couple of days with a farmer and his sons. After an evening of drinking and tale-telling, one of the sons boasted that "even when I cannot see the heavenly bodies, I know the hour of day and night. . . ." The next morning was cloudy with snow flurries, and the king remembered the young man's claim. A sunstone was fetched, and the king found that his young host was right.

Until recently, investigators have paid little attention to the sunstone; but in 1966 archeologist Thorkild Ramskou mentioned it in the magazine *Skalk*. My 12-year-old son showed the article to me. It reminded me at once of the Kollsman Sky Compass which was introduced when the polar airline routes were opened. The Sky Compass essentially is nothing but a piece of polarized glass through which you look at the point directly above you (the zenith); the pattern of polarized sunlight then indicates the direction of the sun.

In a letter to Dr. Ramskou, I explained this, and suggested there might be some natural minerals that would do the same thing. He since has found four minerals that can be used as polarization filters, all of which were available in Scandinavia or Iceland during Viking times: cordierite, andalusite, tourmaline, and Iceland spar. Cordierite, which Dr. Ramskou has used most in his experiments, appears gray until it is rotated into the plane of polarization; then it turns bright blue.

The Scandinavian Airlines System invited Dr. Ramskou to fly with me over waters the Vikings once sailed. He used the sunstone—a piece of cordierite—and I the Sky Compass. Our determinations of direction were almost identical.

That the sunstone was used in Viking navigation is not finally proved. If it was used, it may well have been a closely guarded treasure, known only to kings and their most trusted shipmasters. But just as proof of Norse presence in America waited for us almost a thousand years at L'Anse aux Meadows, so perhaps a sunstone is now waiting in some royal Viking hoard or grave.

With magnificent confidence, the Viking ships—small, elegant, lightly built—plied seas known and unknown, made landfalls friendly and hostile. No one knows how many failed to reach their harbors, but all set out with the fine assumption of getting profitably to their destinations. And so many succeeded!

With well-founded trust in their own skill, intelligence, and courage, the old Norse sailors achieved in shipbuilding and navigation a mastery unequaled in their time.

Index

Illustrations and illustrations references appear in *italics*

Acknowledgments

The Special Publications Division is grateful to the individuals listed here for their assistance during the preparation of this book:

Björn Ambrosiani, Alan Binns, Jacqueline Bozon-Viaille, Stephanie Brodie, H. Bruce Carnall, Lloyd Decker, J. Duhommet, Gísli Gudmundsson, J. S. Hart-Jackson, Tom Henderson, Erling Hole, Hanna Karlsdottir, Benny Kirkegaard, Leif Klepsch, Arne J. Larsen, O. Leroy, Léonce Macary, Odmund Møllerop, Maj Odelberg, J. S. Robshaw, Gunnar Rosvall, Sigurd Simonsen, Sidney R. Smith, Bengt Tengbom, Richard L. Zusi.

Additional Reading

The reader may want to refer to the following books and to check the *National Geographic Index* for related material:

General: Gwyn Jones, *A History of the Vikings;* Bertil Almgren, *The Viking;* Holger Arbman, *The Vikings;* Johannes Brøndsted, *The Vikings;* Peter G. Foote and David M. Wilson, *The Viking Achievement;* P. H. Sawyer, *The Age of the Vikings* (2nd ed.); Jacqueline Simpson, *Everyday Life in the Viking Age.*

Archeology: Sven B. F. Jansson, *The Runes of Sweden;* Haakon Shetelig and Hjalmar Falk, *Scandinavian Archeology* (translated by E. V. Gordon).

Art and Poetry: Lee M. Hollander, *The Skalds;* David M. Wilson and Ole Klindt-Jensen, *Viking Art.*

Ships: A. W. Brøgger and Haakon Shetelig, *The Viking Ships—Their Ancestry and Evolution;* Thorleif Sjøvold, *The Oseberg Find.*

Religion: H. R. Ellis Davidson, *Gods and Myths of Northern Europe;* E. O. G. Turville-Petre, *Myth and Religion of the North.*

Movement East: George Vernadsky, *Ancient Russia* and *Kievan Russia.*

Movement into Europe: Denis Mack Smith, *A History of Sicily: Medieval Sicily;* John Julius Norwich, *The Other Conquest* and *The Kingdom in the Sun;* Earl of Onslow, *The Dukes of Normandy and their Origin;* James Van Wyck Osborne, *The Greatest Norman Conquest;* Francis Palgrave, *The History of Normandy and of England,* vols. I-III; Frank M. Stenton, *Anglo-Saxon England.*

Movement West: Helge Ingstad, *Land under the Pole Star* and *Westward to Vinland;* Gwyn Jones, *The Norse Atlantic Saga;* Knud J. Krogh, *Viking Greenland;* Samuel Eliot Morison, *The European Discovery of America: the Northern Voyages.*

Source Writings: Adam of Bremen, *History of the Archbishops of Hamburg-Bremen* (translated by F. J. Tschan); *The Anglo-Saxon Chronicle* (trans. by G. N. Garmonsway); *The Russian Primary Chronicle* (trans. by S. H. Cross and O. P. Sherbowitz-Wetzor); the Sagas: Jacqueline Simpson, *The Northmen Talk* (excerpts); *Egil's Saga* (trans. by G. Jones); Snorri Sturluson, *Heimskringla* (trans. by L. M. Hollander); Penguin Classics Series: *Njál's Saga, Laxdaela Saga, King Harald's Saga* (all trans. by M. Magnusson and H. Pálsson).

Composition for *The Vikings* by National Geographic's Phototypographic Division, Carl M. Shrader, Chief; Lawrence F. Ludwig, Assistant Chief. Printed and bound by Fawcett Printing Corp., Rockville, Md. Color separations by Graphic Color Plate, Inc., Stamford, Conn.; The Lanman Company, Alexandria, Va.; and Progressive Color Corp., Rockville, Md.